Heart's
Bouquet

By
Louise Barnett Cox

Copyright 1999

Published By

2809 Granny White Pike
Nashville, TN 37204

About The Author

Louise Barnett Cox was born in Albertville, Alabama and raised in Attalla, Alabama. In 1942, she married Charles H. Cox. She graduated from Letcher Business College and finished various college courses in writing, public relations and business.

Louise taught speech on a private basis and had more than 50 years experience in business and industry in the secretarial and administrative assistant fields. After retiring as Administrative Assistant to the Plant Manager of Union Carbide in Cartersville, Georgia, in 1978, she and her husband began working with the Freed-Hardeman College in Henderson, Tennessee. Upon the sickness of Louise's and Charles' mothers, the couple moved back to Alabama to work in Public Relations for Mars Hill Bible School and International Bible College. Following the deaths of both mothers, they returned to Henderson where Louise worked as a part-time church secretary.

Louis Cox spoke at many Ladies' Day Programs and Retreats, College Lectureships and Youth Programs. Her writing included articles in the *Gospel Advocate, Christian Bible Teacher, World Evangelist, F-HC Today*, and *Mars Hill Pacesetters*. Her poetry has been published in *9 to 5* and *Ideals*.

Louise was called home to her Savior on June 11, 1993. Her faith, love, leadership and edification continue in the hearts of those who knew her and loved her—and through their children and friends—and in a special way through this book.

INTRODUCTION

A number of years ago I heard a sermon in which the preacher asked this question, "Are you inviting your friends, neighbors and family to walk with you through a rose garden or through a garden of thorns, thistles and weeds?" Immediately I thought of the verse in John 10:10 where Jesus says, "I come that they might have life and have it more abundantly."

Still later when we moved from Cartersville, Georgia, the congregation made a handmade friendship quilt for us that was most unique. Each square had some creative expression in words or handstitched pictures that would make a long-lasting memory. One of them contained these words:

> "This old world we're living in
> Is mighty hard to beat,
> With every rose you get a thorn,
> But ain't the roses sweet?"

And that's how the idea for this book came to be. God has never promised us a rose garden without thorns, but He has promised us a way to enjoy to roses, despite the thorns. But we must sow well, if we would reap well.

This book is designed to challenge each of us to grow beautiful roses in our lives and share them with everyone we meet for that is abundant living.

DEDICATION

This book is lovingly dedicated to my mother, the late Vida Pittman Barnett, and to my husband, Charles H. Cox. Both of these have helped me to tear down fences, avoid thorns, thistles and weeds in my pathway by inviting me to walk with them through the rose garden of love.

That garden of love for God and others has blossoms that never fade if carefully tended by the instructions given by the Master Gardener in His Word.

TABLE OF CONTENTS

PART I

PLANNING, PREPARING, PLANTING, WEEDING, AND WATERING

TWO GARDENS
by Louise Barnett Cox

I planted a garden against an old rock wall.
I planted for blooming in the spring and the fall.

I watered my garden and nurtured the soil.
I weeded my garden, so naught its bloom would spoil.

I tended my garden with special, loving care.
I planted my garden so I'd have blooms to share.

I carelessly forgot my garden, with so much to do,
And soon I found my garden was hidden from my view.

The weeds grew in my garden thick and strong and tall.
The beauty of my garden withered beside a crumbling wall.

In silence my garden showed the burden I must bear.
It quietly told the world, I simply didn't care!

God planted me in His garden and challenged me to grow.
He wanted me to blossom so Christ's beauty I might show.

I talked with God so often through His Word and prayer
I grew so very close to Him as His Truth I learned to share.

I blossomed in God's garden and I bloomed the whole year 'round.
Wherever I was needed, my loving blossoms were found.

But suddenly I grew careless - I had so much to do.
I left my life untended and I began to wither too.

The weeds choked out my love for God and hid Him from my view
Whene'r I shed a wilting bloom, 'twas a pallid, faded hue.

Sin grew up within me, fierce, and wild and tall
And my beauty died and withered beside the world's decaying wall.

In silence my life shouted the burden I must bear.
It quietly told the world (and God) I simply didn't care.

I took God's planting carelessly and made no move to grow.
My life said, "God doesn't matter" for all the world to know.

HOW DOES YOUR GARDEN GROW?

2

CHAPTER 1

TEAR DOWN THOSE FENCES

Introduction:

Gardens have played an important part in Biblical history. Earthly life began in the Garden of Eden. "And the Lord God planted a garden eastward in Eden; and there he put the man who he had formed." (Gen. 2:8).

The garden of Gethsemene provided the stage for events that made eternal life a reality for those who believe in the Lord, Jesus Christ, and obey His commands. "When Jesus had spoken these words, he went forth with his disciples over the brook of Cedron, where was a garden, into the which he entered and his disciples." (John 18:1). It was here that Judas betrayed our Lord.

If one sees only the death of Jesus at Calvary it is difficult to equate the anguish and suffering of the cross with the beauty of a garden or the promise of eternal life. Yet as we come to see the victory over death and the victory of the death, burial, and resurrection, in all its beauty and fullness of meaning, we can relate it to a beautiful and abundant garden. "Now in the place where he was crucified, there was a garden; and in the garden, a new sepulcher, wherein was man never yet laid. There laid they Jesus therefore because of the Jews' preparation day; for the sepulcher was nigh at hand." (John 19:41-42).

Throughout the Bible we find references to sowing, reaping, planting, pruning, plucking up, growing, being fruitful, differing soils, and harvesting. In our minds are found the "gardens of our hearts" and it is from them that we are sharing either beautiful flowers or thorns, thistles, and weeds.

The following poem of mine was published in Get Well Wishes published by IDEALS many years ago. It was written with someone ill in mind, but it reflects the bouquets we share each day with others.

3

Heart's Bouquet

Though I can't visit you today
To let you know I care,
Still I can send my heart's bouquet
Of love and cheer and prayer.

I'd like to send some sun to you
To make your day more bright
And capture summer's every hue
To add to your delight.

I'd send a bird to sing a song
And add its voice to mine
To say we hope it won't be long
Until you're feeling fine.

Though flowers wilt and soon are gone
Some things will know no end,
And loving thoughts go on and on
In the heart of a faithful friend.

Louise Barnett Cox

Planning For Our Rose Gardens

Life is a series of plantings, cultivating, pruning, weeding, watering, growing and sharing. If we learn to plant the seed of Truth in our heart's gardens, then we will always have beautiful roses to share. But life that is pleasing to God does not just happen, nor do rose gardens. Both take planning. There are many similarities.

Suppose we are planning a rose garden at our home, what would we do?

1. We would look at our lot.

2. We would decide where we wanted the flower garden and what we wanted to plant.

3. If we were cramped for space, we might even want to tear down some fences.

Is planning for the garden of our hearts so different?

First, we need to look at our lot — are we living in God's space or Satan's? Both invite us to plant in their space and reap the rewards they promise. You and I must make the choice.

If we choose to plant in God's space (or choose God's way for our lives), we may have to make some changes. We will, first of all, need to decide whether we will plant roses or weeds. Even if we plant roses in God's space we still have to continue to beware of weeds, but no roses can ever grow in Satan's space.

If our lives are such that we have not put God first then we may (and probably do) have a space far too small for a successful rose garden. Matthew 6:33 gives us the ideal boundary line for starting our garden. Few of us can start without first tearing down some fences. As we tear down the fences, we not only find the space we need for our rose garden, but we open it so those around us may enjoy its beauty.

It was difficult to decide which "fences" to discuss in this book. As you study, you will surely want to add others. The fences are many and varied. Unfortunately, they are far easier to build than they are to tear down.

Tear Down That Fence of Prejudice

Ask yourself the question: "Is there any prejudice in my heart?"

What is prejudice? Someone has described it as "being down on things we are not up on."

It is also (a) preconceived ideas planted so firmly in our minds that we tend to be unwilling to uproot or tear down the fence, and (b) making judgments of anything or anyone before we have all the facts. Matthew 7:1-5 is direct in its opposition to prejudice or pre-judging.

In the interest of time, we shall discuss only a few of the fences of prejudice here.

Racial Prejudice

Do we need to tear down that fence in our lives? As we study these issues, let's think of what "I" need to do in my life, rather than what "they" need to do.

Racial prejudice is found in all races. It breeds a climate of distrust that prohibits the growth of Christian unity in the gardens of our hearts.

Racial prejudice prohibits us from using a highly effective gardening principle. "Therefore, all things whatsoever ye would that men should do to you, do ye even so to them: for this is the law and the prophets." (Matthew 7:12). Furthermore, it violates another specific scripture: "My brethren, have not the faith of our Lord Jesus Christ, the Lord of Glory, with respect of persons." James 2:1. Notice also James 2:9. What are some other scriptures you think of that are violated by racial prejudice?

Ask yourself honestly, "Is there racial prejudice in my heart toward anyone?"

If you need to tear down that fence, one of the best ways is to realize that it can never be destroyed or torn down if we only see things from our own point of view. There are three points of view to be considered: our own - the other fellow's - and God's. If you will read the account of the healing of the blind man in chapter 9 of the book of John, you will see how many different people looked at the same event. None of them saw it fully until they were able to see it from God's point of view. Do you think God has prejudice against any of his creations? Do you think He wants his creation having prejudice against itself?

Often our prejudices are based on "opinions" that we've formed ourselves or that others have passed to us. In the front of a book my late mother gave me when I was a young married woman, she had written these words from an unknown author: "Opinions first, facts last and so confusion. Perhaps someday we will learn to reverse the process and so gain understanding." Prejudice is the end result when we take opinions first and facts last.

If we are willing to let those of a different race look at our rose garden from a distance, but refuse to share with them a heart's bouquet from the garden of love, then we are racially prejudiced whether we admit it or not and not pleasing to God accordingly.

Money is essential in our lives, but it can be a force for good or a force for evil. Money in and of itself, is not wrong or evil. Our attitude toward it may be evil. I have noted highly visible evidence of materialistic prejudice within various congregations of the Lord's Church. It is something that is rarely voiced, but often reflected in both actions and attitudes.

Have you ever seen those with money look down on those without? Have you ever noted how much difference may be made in a well-dressed visitor and one who is poorly dressed? If you can see a difference, then fences need to be torn down if roses are to bloom within the Lord's church. Discuss James 2:1-9. Discuss the verse of scripture that reads, "For the love of money is the root of all evil; which while some coveted after, they have erred from the faith, and pierced themselves through with many sorrows" (I Timothy 6:10). In what ways does the love of money become the root of all kinds of evil?

But the rich are not the only ones guilty of materialistic prejudice. Note the mention of "coveted" in the scripture referred to above. Covetousness can build high fences in the lives of those with money and without money. Often the poor feel envy, jealousy, resentment and even hatred for those who are wealthy in their eyes. They covet what the other person has to the point that their fence of discontent makes it impossible for them to recognize that they can grow roses in their hearts if they choose, for God's roses are not bought with money; they are a labor of love, love for God and man.

Covetousness, which means to desire ardently or to crave, helps us to build fences that make those with money feel self-sufficient or to be so blind to the needs of others that they can ignore them completely. But it can also cause discontent, envy and hatred to eat away at the poor until they become blinded to many of the blessings that they already enjoy.

This is not God's way. Ephesians 5:3 lists covetousness along with "fornication and all uncleanness" as not being "becoming to saints." Verse 5 states plainly that covetousness is idolatry.

If we would tear down those fences of materialistic prejudice, then we must realize the wisdom of praying as did Solomon in Proverbs 30:8-9 as an effective tool in tearing down materialistic fences. "Remove far from me vanity and lies; give me neither poverty nor riches; feed me with food convenient for me; lest I be full and deny thee and say, Who is the Lord? or lest I be poor and steal, and take the name of my God in vain."

Intellectual Prejudice

Have you noticed that every fence we build through prejudice has two sides?

Another fence that is being built higher and higher is that of intellectual prejudice. On the one side many who are highly educated look down on the men and women with little or no education and do not see them as persons of value in God's kingdom. On the other hand, many who have less education often direct criticism and distrust at those who hold advanced degrees.

Discuss how these fences can create problems in blooming as God would have us bloom in the garden space He has planned for us to use. How does I Corinthians 1:18-31 apply at this point?

Perhaps an understanding of Proverbs 1:2-7 will give us tools, such as wisdom, justice, and equity that we all need to tear down the fences of intellectual prejudice. The sharpest tool of all is found in Proverbs 1:7, "The fear of the Lord is the beginning of knowledge; but fools despise wisdom and instruction."

Jesus set the example in Luke 2:52 for our four-way growth pattern - wisdom, stature, favor with God and man. Lack of wisdom can make the most highly educated or the poorest educated man or woman small in stature and keep them from the favor of God or man. Fences must be torn down if roses are to bloom.

But there are other fences.

8

Tear Down the Fences of Guilt

Because we are not and will never be perfect on this earth, we often carry a burden of guilt. We build a fence of guilt that blinds us to the grace of God. We tend to see God as we may be ourselves — incapable of forgiving.

What is the first step in tearing down a fence of guilt to give ourselves more space to grow beautiful roses? "For if ye forgive men their trespasses, your heavenly Father will also forgive you; But if ye forgive not men their trespasses, neither will your Father forgive your trespasses." (Matthew 6:14-15).

The fences of guilt are built of highly expensive materials -unforgiving and impenitent hearts. It takes real effort to tear them down, but with God's help, all things are possible.

When we refuse to forgive a brother or sister or ourselves, we set ourselves above God. He can forgive, but we are saying we can't. When we are unwilling to repent of our sins and seek forgiveness we are like a withered rose losing its petals. If we seek God's forgiveness, but refuse to forgive ourselves, then the roses in life's garden will wither and die from lack of space and air.

When we assume that what we have done is too bad for God to forgive, then we attempt to make God a liar and Jesus of no effect. The death on the cross set the terms for forgiveness. We cannot draw up our own terms. When we do, we merely build higher fences.

One reason we have difficulty forgiving ourselves may be our attitude toward our forgiveness of others. We say we forgive, but continue to watch and whisper behind their backs. We play detective, hoping to catch them making a mistake. We continue to hold them at arm's length, instead of treating them as brothers and sisters in Christ. As we attempt to smother the roses in their gardens by our unforgiving spirit, we are also failing to give the roses in our gardens space in which to grow.

How do we tear down that fence of guilt? We do so only by putting our trust in God in all things and not in ourselves. We cannot seek the kingdom of God and his righteousness first (Matt. 6:33) until we learn to tear down the fences of guilt.

How much we need the help of one another in both the matter of forgiveness and the matter of tearing down the fence of guilt in our lives.

Tear Down the Fence of Selfishness.

Would you agree that most of us have built more fences of selfishness than any other fence? We build fences — although called by other names — from the materials of our own personal selfishness. In discussing this book with friends of mine, I asked which fence they found most difficult to tear down. The answer was the same each time, "Selfishness, for it is that which prompts the building of most of the other fences." Do you agree or disagree?

The fences of selfishness come in many different styles, but each of them diminishes the space for growing our rose garden. Most of them seem to carry a highly visible sign that reads, "THIS IS MINE. KEEP OUT."

Let's use some scriptures to see just how the fence of selfishness can keep us from having the needed space for a bountiful rose garden. It kept Eve from enjoying the garden of Eden; it does the same for us today.

Matthew 6:33: How can we seek God first when our selfishness demands that we put ourselves and our personal desires above everything and everyone else? If selfishness is a high fence in our lives, is it not also true that much of the goods we have accumulated or positions we have attained may have been gained at the expense of others? Discuss. What are some attitudes that are representative of the world in which we live today that encourage a selfishness that would make it difficult to share our heart's bouquet of love with any one?

Matthew 22:37-39: It is impossible to give real love from a selfish heart. God's command is that we love Him with all our heart, soul, mind and strength, and our neighbor as ourselves. Why is selfishness a fence that prevents us from loving God, our neighbor or ourselves as God commands? Selfishness eventually destroys all meaningful relationships and eventually destroys us. A recent survey of hospitals and nursing homes indicated that the more selfish an individual, the longer the recovery period. Should this be surprising news to one who believes God's word? I think not.

II Peter 1:5-11: A bountiful rose garden in our yard or in our hearts must have growth. The beautiful pattern for spiritual growth is found in this scripture. But when the fence of selfishness encloses our gardens there is not space for such growth. There is no faith in selfishness; there is no virtue (courage) in selfishness, only fear that our personal desires will not be met. There is no knowledge in selfishness for it denies the scriptures and crucifies Jesus afresh. There is no temperance in selfishness for it is built upon the excess of personal desires. Selfishness lacks patience. Selfishness and godliness cannot live in the same garden for they are directly opposed to one another. Selfishness causes us to be so wrapped up in our own selves that we are unaware of our family and our brothers and sisters in Christ, so how can we treat them with brotherly kindness? There is no real charity (love) in selfishness, only the destructive and deceptive love of self. Discuss.

Conclusion:

Are we willing to tear down those fences in our lives so that we may have bountiful gardens to share with others? Or are we content to live in the crowded space behind the fences and walk daily through the area as we fight our way through thorns, thistles and weeds?

There are no shortcuts for tearing down fences. It takes time, effort and hard work. Without Christ it is impossible. But Philippians 4:13 tells us "I can do all things through Christ which strengtheneth me." I believe that includes tearing down the highest of fences. We cannot hire someone else to tear down our fences. They were not built in a day; nor will they be torn down in a day. But until the fences are down, there is no space for our roses of love to prosper so that we may share our heart's bouquet as God intends.

Perhaps you are thinking, "Who does she think she is?" "How can she tell me all this? She is no wiser than I am." You are right. I am simply a woman who has built and torn down many fences (and continue to do so). But I promise you that each time I have torn down a fence I have found that not only is "the grass greener on the other side of the fence," the roses are also sweeter and more beautiful.

FOR THOUGHT AND DISCUSSION

1. What is the difference between the "abundant life" referred to in John 10:10 and the "affluence" which we often confuse with abundant living?

2. What are some other fences not mentioned in our lesson that we might need to tear down in our lives to have space for our rose garden?

3. Can you give Biblical, historical or current examples of people who have fenced themselves in by prejudice, guilt, or selfishness?

4. Why is it often easier for us to recognize a neighbor's fence that needs to be torn down than it is to recognize our own?

5. Are you willing to share with the class something you have done personally or some scripture that has helped you to tear down a fence?

6. Find three scriptures that if applied to our lives would make our lives more beautiful both here and hereafter?

   a. _____

   b. _____

   c. _____

7. We have often heard the quotation "God has not promised us a rose garden." Is it not possible to think that God might use us to share with others a heart's bouquet from the gardens of our hearts? Why or why not?

FOR YOUR PERSONAL USE

Unless we take Bible principles and commands outside the classroom and make application to our own lives, we are losing something of great value. This is for each of us to think about personally and privately during the days following this lesson.

Take the Test
Do You Have Space Enough to Build That Rose Garden?

How would you like to make an "A" on this test? I am going to give you five "A's" that may help you to tear down fences in your life, but also do well on this test.

AWARENESS: Are you *aware* of any fences in your own life? Think about it seriously and list them. Then list fences you see in the lives of your family and friends. Is there any difference? What do the lists tell you?

ATTITUDE: What is your *attitude* toward your own fences compared to the fences in the lives of others? Which is greater "the mote or the beam?" Is there any difference between your attitude toward your own fences and God's attitude toward them.

ATTENTION: Are you willing to give close *attention* to applying the scriptures to your life as a means of tearing down the fences you find? Use your concordance to find scriptures that relate to the fences you are trying to tear down. Would you be willing to ask for help if you needed it, or would you be willing to help another if asked?

ACCEPTANCE: Are you willing to *accept* the fact that, even as Christians, we will have problems, temptations, and sorrows? But will you ALSO ACCEPT the fact that, with God's help, you can tear down every fence and give your roses room to grow? Will you accept the fact that planting in God's garden means going His way and not yours?

ACTION: Will you take *action* every day you live to tear down fences and carve paths of righteousness and faith through the thorns, thistles and weeds so that you may enjoy the beauty of abundant rose garden of Christian living. . . and invite others to share it with you?

Will you take the ACTION you need to take to make the sign "In Christ there is endless hope, without him a hopeless end" more than just a sign, but a way of life for you?

MY PRAYER FOR YOU

Dear Heavenly Father, how wonderful it is to know that wherever there are those studying or reading this book and seeking to enjoy the beauty of Christian living by YOUR pattern, YOU are there with them.

Give us wisdom, courage and strength to tear down our fences. Give us willing hearts that the roses of faith, truth, love, and concern for others may bloom abundantly in our lives.

Forgive us, Father, when we fall short, as we so often do. Help us to forgive others and ourselves as we ask you to forgive us.

Thank you, God, for the beautiful plan you designed for us to live in the garden of life here on earth and in Heaven with you when this life is over. Help us to make the choices to insure such blessings.

Thank you, Father, for your Son, who was willing to die for us. May each of us be willing to live for Him. It is in His dear name we pray.

Amen

CHAPTER 2

PREPARING THE SOIL

Introduction:

If you and I want to plant roses in the garden of our heart so that we may share our "Heart's Bouquet" with those around us, we must first prepare the soil.

The soil in which we plant roses, truths, or attitudes is of vital importance to the quality of our garden. It even makes a difference as to whether a seed germinates or a plant grows to maturity. All good gardeners know the value of proper soil and soil preparation.

Luke 8:4-15 is a graphic illustration of how the seed of God's Word may be sown in different kinds of soil with totally different results, although the seed is always the same.

In preparation for the study of this chapter let's sit quietly for a moment and think about the quality of the soil in our own hearts.

Is the seed being planted in our heart's gardens falling by the way side so that it is carried away by every wind of doctrine? Are we influenced more by the attitudes of the world than by the desire to share the blossoms from our heart's garden and have a positive influence in the world around us?

Or is the seed planted in a rocky soil? Did it spring up fitfully, then wither and die because it lacked the moisture needed to bring it to maturity?

Was the seed sown in our hearts and then when the trials and temptations came along, they were as thorns that choked out the seed?

Or has the seed fallen on the good ground of a loving and receptive heart that it may grow and become a beautiful bouquet of the heart to be shared in many ways with many people?

Only we and God know the condition of our heart's soil. Most of us need to do some soil preparation if we want our heart's bouquet to be as beautiful as God intended it to be.

This chapter will look at soil preparation through the use of three soil nutrients. As you have meditated upon the soil in your own heart, you will know how best to use these nutrients to enrich your heart's soil to insure an abundance of roses that may be shared in your heart's bouquet.

Preparing the Soil Through Bible Study

As I talk with women's groups throughout the country, I am often confronted with the question, "How can I find time for Bible study?" I do not believe we FIND time. I believe we must MAKE time. I cannot give a foolproof formula for making the time, each of us must use the method that works best for us.

Instead of a formula, I will share some ideas that have been shared with me:

(1)   "Until I came to accept the fact that II Timothy 2:15 meant God wanted me to study to be approved of him, I could not find the time to study. Once I accepted that fact, then I changed my priorities." said a middle-aged woman.

(2)   A young mother with several small children said, "When I read my children a Bible study at night I go to the scriptures and find the basis for the story and all of us memorize a verse from those scriptures. Then we have a prayer. This has been a good source of Bible study for me at this time in my life. The points made for children in the stories often are most helpful to me."

(3)   An elderly woman said, "Now that I have more time that is unscheduled, I find I can't see as well, so I still have to use my time for Bible study wisely in order to get the most out of it."

(4)   A young wife who runs a home and also a career said, "My husband and I walk or jog each morning or each evening. We each have a tape recorder with ear phones so we listen to tapes as we exercise. We have tapes of the Bible and listen to the same portion and then discuss it when we get home."

(5)   A woman who has the most hectic household I have ever seen laughs as she says, "The only time there is peace and quiet for me at home is when I go to the bathroom, so I keep my Bible and other study materials there so that I can claim a few minutes out of each day to study and pray undisturbed.

(6)   My husband, Charles, and I share an early morning devotional and study time together. We get up an hour earlier than is necessary in order to do this.

Perhaps you have ways of claiming time for Bible study that you would like to share.

When, where and how we study are not the important issues for preparing the soil of our hearts. The major issue is that Bible study is something we do regularly and for a purpose, rather than now and then as a duty.

You may study an outline, a book such as this with scripture references, a topical study, verse by verse, characters of the Bible, events, a book of the Bible at a time. The important thing is that no matter when and how you study, if your attitude is right, the soil of your heart is enriched and the roses will bloom for your heart's bouquet.

Preparing the Soil Through Prayer

Use your concordance and find three scriptures that relate to prayer. Discuss them as a class.

Nothing I do prepares my heart to be more receptive to the will of God than my prayer life. Something else may do more for you to enrich the soil of your heart than prayer. But prayer is very special to me.

Here are some reasons why. Prayer is a wonderful privilege granted to me, a Christian woman, by my Heavenly Father. There is no need to worry, God will hear my prayer if I pray in accordance with His will. Have you ever felt the need to talk with someone confidentially and immediately? Perhaps you want to talk with your husband or a friend. You dial their office and the line is busy. Or they say they are busy at the moment and will call you back. Or perhaps whoever answers the phone says, "Let me put you on hold while I locate them." You wait and wait and wait, and finally the voice says, "I can't seem to locate them. Could you call back later or would you like to leave a message?" Isn't it wonderful that God is never too busy to hear our prayers even though thousands of people are praying at the very same instant? God never puts us on hold, day or night. He is there when we need him.

Often we feel hesitant to pray because we feel we don't know what to say, but Jesus is making intercession for us, and God hears our prayers no matter how inadequately we may word them. Once when I was growing up, my brother offered a prayer at mealtime, and I said, "You talked so low I couldn't hear you." He said, "I wasn't talking to you. I was talking to God." God hears a whispered prayer, if it is in accordance with His will.

Have you ever been grateful that God listened to your prayer and then gave you what was best for you instead of exactly what you asked for? So many times God has answered my prayers "Yes", or "No", or "Wait awhile" and the best answer of all is "I have something better in mind for you."

When we pray do we merely ask or do we remember to thank God? We should not pray to be seen or heard of men, but are we ashamed to pray? I remember once soon after I was married we were eating in a nice restaurant and my husband, as is his custom, bowed his head and began to pray before our meal. When it was over I said, "You know we could bow our heads and pray silently, you don't have to pray out loud." I shall never forget his reply, "That's right, God, don't you give me any blessings when anyone is looking. You just wait until I am alone so no one will know."

Have you ever thought of what a privilege we have praying in our ladies' classes? Many years ago an elderly lady chastised me for praying in a ladies' class I was teaching, saying that women should not pray - even when only women are present. I remember asking her if she had gone to the hospital to visit a dear friend who was near death and that friend said, "Please pray for me that I will have the courage to face death unafraid," what she would do. I asked, "Would you say, 'I don't know how?' Would you say, 'Let me go get a preacher or an elder or some man. You see, I can't pray. I don't know how.'"

Fear often keeps us from praying in our ladies' class. Once I asked a lady on Sunday if she would lead our opening prayer in class Wednesday. She said, "I can't. I never have." I asked her, "Do you want to come to the end of your life and realize that never once have you prayed with your sisters in Christ?" She thought a moment and said, "I'll do it." She prayed a meaningful prayer for all of us and has thanked me many times for pointing her to a God-given privilege that she had neglected far too long.

When we move through life in the fast-pace of the present century, we often forget that the scriptures tell us of our need to "be still and know that he is God." (Psalm 46:10) Few things of a spiritual nature which we do can draw us any nearer to God than our private prayers that come from our hearts. No wonder they prepare the soils of our hearts to so readily accept the seed of the Word and let it grow unhampered in a willing and a loving heart.

A final thought along this line. If we would give to another a heart's bouquet from our garden of love, what better way than just the simple statement, "You are in my prayers." What a beautiful privilege to be able to pray for one another.

Examine your prayer life and see if it is such that your heart is becoming more fertile because of the nutrients that come from an open communication with God — a communication that is nothing more than that of a child, in simple, trusting faith, asking the Father for needs, guidance, forgiveness and love.

Preparing the Soil Through Worship

What is the purpose of the worship services of the church? God has no need of our worship, but our lives are enriched in ways too numerous to mention when we worship in spirit and in truth.

Locate (using your concordance) at least five scriptures that relate to New Testament worship. Read and discuss.

The purpose of this lesson is to help each of us discover how to make the worship service more meaningful and how to live lives that are in praise, reverence and honor to the Lord.

What is worship? Among other things it is tendering reverence and honor to God. As previously stated, God does not need our worship, but we, as humans, have a deep seated need to worship. It has been said that man will worship **something**. When that worship is directed toward our Maker and is done with understanding in spirit and in truth, it becomes a learning and growing experience for each of us. It is soil preparation in every sense of the word.

Before we look at what constitutes worship. Let's consider some things worship is **not**.

1. Worship is not a spectator sport which we are to watch in a detached sort of way.

2. Worship is not a disorderly event in which we are each free to "do our own things."

3. Worship, while it is to be orderly, is not a cold ritual which we go through in routine fashion.

4. Worship — in any of its segments — is not a performance on our part.

5. Worship is not a matter of choice, it is a command of God.

New Testament worship is the expression of our love, reverence, honor and praise to God and to our savior, Jesus Christ. It is a privilege, a blessing and a command. It is a learning and growing activity for all who will permit it to be. It is a coming together for a common purpose that will strengthen each of us, as we unite in love, praise and reverence for our Lord.

New Testament worship follows the pattern set by the church in the first century. We as individuals participate in the worship in the following ways: singing, praying (as we silently pray along with the person leading the prayer), hearing the Word of God preached, giving, and partaking of the Lord's Supper as we remember not only His death on the cross but also His resurrection and His coming again. During no part of the worship may we can remain detached and really worship.

Look at these scriptures that relate to the items of worship (add others as you choose and discuss).

Singing: I Corinthians 14:15, Colossians 3:16

Praying: Colossians 3:17, Mark 11:24

Preaching: II Timothy 4:2, II Corinthians 4:5

Giving: I Corinthians 16:1-2; II Corinthians 9:6-9

Lord's Supper: I Corinthians 11:24-25

Now ask yourself if you truly worship when you attend a worship service. Can you sing "Purer in Heart" in a worshipful manner while you harbor envy, resentment or intense dislike for someone? Can you sing "I Want to Be a Worker For the Lord" and refuse to become involved in the work of the church without singing a lie?

Can you pray sincerely from a bitter and unforgiving heart? Can you pray sincerely from an impenitent heart?

If, during the sermon, you are wondering if the roast left on at home is burning, are you truly worshipping? If you are gazing around to see what everyone is wearing, are you worshipping? If you are intently listening for the speaker to make a grammatical error so you can be critical later, are you worshipping in spirit and in truth? If you pass the preacher on your way out and say, "Good sermon," and he asks, "What did I preach about?", would you have worshipped properly if you have not the vaguest idea? What about during the week? Shouldn't every sermon you hear make some difference in your life?

As you partake of the Lord's Supper, if you do it in a mechanical and routine fashion with no thought of its meaning, have you worshipped?

Are you giving like Ananias and Sapphira or like the widow who gave a mite? Discuss. Are you giving in a worshipful and grateful manner if you fumble in your purse to find something to drop in the plate without purposing or thinking of your blessings?

The scriptures list three very different types of worship.

Vain Worship - Matthew 15:9
Ignorant Worship - Acts 17:23
Worship in Spirit and in truth - John 4:21-24

Each of us worships in one of these ways. God knows into which category our worship falls. If our worship is vain or ignorant then the soil of our heart is not right. During the invitation at the worship service is a wonderful time to make a commitment to enrich the soil by repenting, asking for forgiveness, and doing whatever it takes to make the soil preparation complete enough to plant the roses of God's love in it. (Of course, one need not wait until then; now while you are reading this would be an even better time!)

Let us not forget that the honor, love, praise and gratitude we owe God and Christ cannot be fulfilled during a worship service alone. Our lives must reflect the fact that the purpose of them is to let a world see Christ living in us. Read carefully the words to the familiar hymn "My Task" and you will find a pattern for living that will glorify God, reflect Christ and enrich the heart's soil. It is a word picture of sharing our heart's bouquet with others, not for our glory, but for the glory of God.

FOR THOUGHT AND DISCUSSION

1. Discuss meaningful ways you have found to improve your personal Bible study.

2. Mention some people and some things for which the class needs to pray. Have someone lead such a prayer.

3. What are some interferences that make it difficult for you to have a worshipful attitude during a service?

4. What are some things that could be done to improve an individual's attitude toward worship? What could we do to prevent it from becoming a ritual?

FOR YOUR PERSONAL USE

Try this as a means of getting more out of the worship service by putting more into it.

1. As you sing, make a note of the titles so that you can perhaps read the words when you go home. Listen to the words as you sing and make them a personal message to YOU, not just words of a poet set to music.

2. Lose yourself in prayer. Don't let your mind wander. Pray silently with the person leading the prayer. When the prayer is over, pray silently to God that he will help you to put heart, hands and feet to those prayers. Pray as if everything depended on God; but work as if everything depended on you.

3. Make notes during the sermon. Review them during the week and put them to work in the soil preparation for your heart's garden. Share something from the sermon with someone else during the week.

4. Rid your mind of all thoughts except Jesus Christ as you partake of the Lord's Supper. Think of the agony of the cross, think of the love it reflects; think and visualize the resurrection and think of the hope it gives to us that we may know victory in Jesus; think of Christ's coming again and how glorious it will be for those who are ready and how tragic it will be for those who are unprepared.

5. Count your blessings as you purpose to give.

6. Enjoy the fact that you live in a country where you are free to worship without fear. Enjoy the wonderful privilege of meeting together with your brothers and sisters in Christ to worship your Creator and your Saviour.

MY PRAYER FOR YOU

Our loving Heavenly Father. We love you so much. Help us to appreciate the wonderful ways in which you have provided us with spiritual nutrients to enrich the soil of our heart.

May we come to know thy will that we may better do it. Thank you for the Bible which reveals it to us. May we study in a way that will help us to grow spiritually.

Thank you for the avenue of prayer that we are privileged to enjoy. Thank you for the many prayers you have answered. Thank you for your wisdom that gives us what we need and not always that for which we ask. Help us to know the joy of communicating with you in prayer.

Dear Father, thank you for the privilege of worshipping you. May we do so in spirit and truth and from a sense of love and not duty. Thank you, Father, for the gift of your Son. Help us to glorify all that this gift reflects by the lives we live.

Forgive us and help us to prepare the soil of our hearts to receive thy Word with love, joy, hope and obedience. In Jesus' name.

Amen

CHAPTER 3

PLANTING SEEDS OF KNOWLEDGE TO
REAP A HARVEST OF WISDOM

Introduction:

No matter how much we wish to grow beautiful roses in the garden at our home or the roses of love within our hearts, nothing is going to happen until the seed is planted.

If it is roses we want, we will not plant sunflower seeds regardless of how much we like sunflowers. If it is love of God and our fellowman that we want, we will plant the Word of God in our hearts, regardless of the attractive way in which sin may be portrayed to us.

The purpose of this lesson is to look at how the seeds of knowledge may be planted through Bible study, both in private and class settings.

If this is a class study, have the class sing the hymn "Give Me The Bible," and read the following scriptures: Hosea 4:6, Isaiah 40:7-8, Psalm 119:105, II Timothy 2:15-16, II Timothy 3:16-17. Then have someone lead a prayer for wisdom. It is only when we are able to turn our knowledge into wisdom that the seeds take root, grow, and bloom.

How to Plant

Even if the planting is done in the framework of a ladies' Bible class, there is still need for much private Bible study. But let's look first at the Bible class study. As I have taught ladies' classes and spoken to ladies' groups for many years I have discovered that "how we plant" is as important as "what we plant."

I believe that most of the women I know fall into one of the following four categories:

(1) *Lazy Planters.* I find far too many women (and also teachers who encourage it) who are content to be spoon-fed by someone else. All too often this group will buy whatever is being taught — truth, error, opinion, or even dissension. They tend to disregard the admonitions of the scriptures to "buy the TRUTH and sell it not" and to "prove all things." Seeds planted by the handsful, rather than painstakingly scattered rarely grow to maturity.

(2) *Hypocritical Planters.* Although I believe this number is small, I believe it is dangerous. These are the women who attend a Bible class, but are bored by it. Away from class they ridicule teacher, materials, even the Word of God, and rebel against it in secret. They may openly admit (to close acquaintances) that they do what the scriptures tell them, but they long to be involved in things of the world. This group of women want to be entertained and amused, not informed and improved. They long to be "of the world" and ignore the warning that says "come ye out from among them." They are far more impressed by what man has to say than by what the Word of God has to say.

A friend of mine relates speaking to a large ladies' class for a semester and noting that when she read or quoted from something other than the Bible she had their rapt attention. But when she read from the Bible she felt she lost them instantly. This was not representative of the entire class, but of a small and highly visible group. They were like someone planting sunflower seeds in the hopes of growing roses. But the most tragic thing is that women in this group are often prominent in many activities and their influence falls like constant shadow on newly sown seed and stunts the growth.

3. *Know-It-All Planters.* Another small group whose seed may never germinate are those who "appear knowledgeable." They can quote (and usually do so loudly) many scriptures and Bible facts. They like to impress others with their knowledge. They frequently are highly critical of others. They know the facts, but not what to do with them. They have a "zeal but not according to knowledge." Their hearts are but storage bins for the seed of knowledge, rather than gardens where knowledge of the Word of God becomes wisdom that lives and grows abundantly.

4. *Approved Planters.* How exciting are those women who are studying to show themselves approved unto God. They enjoy the adventure of Bible study. They are women who are receptive to the fact that we never learn all there is to know from the Bible, nor do we reach the point where study is not necessary. They seek to understand how to APPLY what they have learned. It becomes a pattern for their planting so that the roses of love bloom abundantly for the heart's bouquets they wish to share with others. Their beauty does not fade.

Think for a moment. Into which group do you fit? No one needs know but you and God. God already knows, but perhaps you have not before recognized the group into which you fit.

When we are in any group other than Group 4 we need to consider trying new methods of planting properly so that knowledge may truly become wisdom. In a class I was teaching, one of the members made this statement, "What good does it do for my child to know that two and two make four, if she does not know that she and God equal everything?" So it is with our knowledge. We can know all the facts, quote verse after verse of scripture, but until we make Truth come alive in our lives, it is of little profit.

It is interesting to note that no matter what one's attitude toward Truth may be, it will not change or destroy Truth. Our poor attitudes only change and/or destroy ourselves and others.

Dangers of Improper Planting

If in our planting we use the wrong kind of food, or too little or too much, we should not be surprised if what we plant suffers from malnutrition and has severe growth problems. If you are following the advice of the world in seeking nutrients for your spiritual planting, you will find your spiritual harvest lacking. What are some of the influences of the world which may hinder your harvest?

But even if you are content to have a minister, an elder, a husband, a parent, teacher or friend do the feeding of your planting, there is always the possibility that there will be a lack because it has not received your personal attention. Your plants may be receiving the equivalent of a milk diet when what is needed is the equivalent of meat. Paul pointed out (Hebrews 5:12-14) that you have to desire "the sincere milk of the word" before you are ready for meat. In your planting, you must be sure that the proper order of feeding, using the proper kind and amount of nutrients, is carried out to get the maximum production of blossoms for your heart's bouquet.

Just as improper planting will destroy the development of our roses, so does a wrong attitude toward Bible study. Our Bible study and our reaction to it is a personal thing. It CANNOT be done for us by someone else. Being content to be spoon-fed is a dangerous thing. There IS a better way. For example, read and discuss: Acts 17:11; I Thessalonians 5:21; Hebrews 5:12-14.

If we fall into the group who have no sincere interest in God's Word and often use it merely to argue foolishly and disrupt a class, we are dangerous to ourselves and to others. These women are often very opinionated and seek to force their opinions on others. Their rebellion against the scriptures may lead them to ridicule Bible principles and moral values as old-fashioned and out-of-date. Such women may resent all forms of authority and consider themselves a law unto themselves.

Read II Timothy 4:2-5, Matthew 7:13, Proverbs 14:1, II Timothy 2:16; and I Corinthians 3:19 and discuss them in connection with this group of hypocritical Bible students.

"Pride goeth before a fall" and so it is with women who take pride in their Bible knowledge. The real seeker of Truth knows that the more one learns, the more one realizes how much he or she needs to learn. Few things can stunt our growth more than a pride in our own spiritual maturity. Locate scripture references that indicate our need to be humble, not to think more highly of ourselves than we should, and that we are incapable of directing our own steps. Read and discuss.

The Bible study class was never intended to replace our private Bible study. But it can enhance it. Trying to reap a harvest of wisdom without taking advantage of various and different opportunities to study God's Word is like hoping to gather roses from our gardens when we've never planted any.

Advantages of Planting the Seeds of Knowledge in a Ladies Bible Class

Most of us are fortunate enough to be able to attend Bible classes on Sunday and Wednesday. These classes may be of both men and women, or they may be classes that we are called upon to teach. Sometimes they may be classes for ladies only. We can plant seeds of knowledge in our lives through any of these classes, yet I believe the greatest opportunity we have to do serious planting is in the ladies' class.

I hope that you have opportunity to attend a ladies' class that is held sometime other than on Sunday morning or Wednesday night. It is a great opportunity for learning what to do with what you have learned. Many of these extra classes may have more time and opportunity for practical application of our Bible knowledge.

Now that so many women are working outside the home, it is often difficult for them to attend such a class. Yet they may have a very deep need for such an opportunity. Here are three examples of how others have handled such a problem:

1. One lady I know set up a noontime session which she called "The Brown Bag Ladies' Bible Class." Each attendee brought her lunch in a brown bag and they had their class as they ate. This provided opportunity to invite their co-workers. It proved highly successful.

2. Another congregation I know has the class on a Tuesday evening so that working women can attend.

3. Still another woman I know asked for permission to take her lunch hour at 9:30 so that she could attend the weekly ladies' class.

Where there's a will there's a way.

What are some of the advantages for the ladies' classes of these types? They are usually taught by a woman, and so the material is less general and more specific in areas in which women need strengthening.

They provide opportunity for class members to lead in prayer, give devotionals, teach a segment of the lesson, or ask questions, serve on a panel or give special reports. It is "knowledge being put to work to become wisdom" when women have opportunity to use their talents to help in the class.

They also provide opportunity for Christian fellowship. This ishighly meaningful in our transient society where so frequently families find themselves in communities where they know no one and have no roots. Perhaps this little story I heard brother C.W. Bradley tell will illustrate our need for other Christians in our lives as well as for planting well.

Brother Bradley says, "It was the night after a severe windstorm in Memphis. When I arrived at the church building that morning, I found one tree blown down completely, torn up by the roots. Yet beyond that tree were a number of other trees that were untouched by the fury of the storm. Puzzled, I studied the situation more closely and here is what I discovered about the tree that was blown down:

1. It was top heavy — all its branches were up near the top instead of being well-balanced as the other trees were.

2. Its roots did not go very deep so it had little or no foundation to keep it intact.

3. It stood all alone and lacked the support of the other trees to protect it from the storm.

"How like that tree we Christians are. If we do not have a good spiritual balance in our lives we become top heavy. When our roots of spiritual growth are not well grounded in Truth we can easily be toppled. We need the fellowship and encouragement of other Christians to help us withstand the storms of life." So in order that we may have the protection and support of other Christians, we need to seek out Christian fellowship.

The ladies' class also provides opportunity for service and until our knowledge leads us in avenues of service to both God and man, it has not yet become wisdom.

What are at least six areas of service that can be rendered by the members of a ladies' Bible class? How are we planting?

FOR THOUGHT AND DISCUSSION

1. What are some topics that need to be addressed in a ladies' Bible class?

2. How can a class be designed to meet the needs of women of all ages and specific needs?

3. There is a need for more women to write Bible-oriented material for use in a ladies' class. Do you know of someone who could write such material, but isn't doing do? Encourage her to do so.

4. What are some special benefits you gain from your own ladies' Bible class?

5. How can you encourage more women to become involved?

FOR YOUR PERSONAL USE

Try to become excited over the study of the Bible.

Think what it would be like if you were not permitted to own a Bible or assemble for study and worship.

Try to bring to class something you have learned from a use of the scriptures that will relate to what you are studying.

If you memorize just one verse of scripture each day, at the end of a year you would know 365 scriptures from memory.

If you apply just one verse of scripture to your life each day, you will be unable to keep from sharing your HEART'S BOUQUET with someone you meet along the way.

Remember what an unknown writer said, "If you INHALE enough of the word of God, you'll have to EXHALE it."

GIFT WRAPPING MY DAY

When at the start of each new day
I take time to read God's Word and pray,
I remain amazed at the strength I gain
To handle joy, success or trials and pain.

I find the courage to run each day's race
And fill contentedly my own special place
That God has planned for me alone to fill,
As I seek to know and ever do His will.

When at the end of each departed day,
I take time to read God's Word and pray
I'm grateful for God's gift to me.
He gift-wrapped this entire day, you see.

Louise Barnett Cox

MY PRAYER FOR YOU

Dear Heavenly Father, thank you for the gift of life. Let us live it in a way that is pleasing to Thee. Thank you for the freedom we enjoy to study, pray and serve without fear. Help us to grasp each opportunity gratefully and plant the seeds of knowledge at each opportunity so that we may reap harvest of wisdom that can be your gift to us if we but seek it. In Jesus' name we pray.

Amen

CHAPTER 4

DON'T PLANT POISON IVY
IN YOUR ROSE GARDEN

Introduction:

My husband thinks this is a ridiculous topic. He asks, "Who would plant poison ivy in a rose garden?" I agree that no one would intentionally do so. But what if someone did not recognize what she was planting until it had "taken over?"

One of the descriptions in the dictionary is "any of several American Sumacs of somewhat vine-like habit with herbage poisoning to touch." I recall my parents cautioning me, as a child, to watch for the three leaves by which I could identify poison ivy. I also recall the painful and ugly results for children who had not been so warned, or who had ignored warnings.

I believe this is a practical analogy. Too often the poison ivy of sin in our lives is not recognized for what it is until it has taken a firm hold in our lives. We may not have been warned against it, or taught to identify sin in all its various shapes: or we may choose to ignore warnings. We may be as children, playing innocently with what seems harmless and even attractive. We fail to recognize danger.

That's what this chapter is about: how to identify the poison ivy of sin and refuse to plant it in the gardens of our hearts. But also to help others learn to identify and rid themselves of the dangerous growth.

Identification and Protection

Just as my parents taught me to identify and protect myself from poison ivy, so God, through His Word and the example of Jesus Christ, teaches us to identify specifically three leaves of temptation and the reliable method of protection.

Few people die as a result of poison ivy. But the Bible is clear in its warnings of the deadliness of sin in our lives. Romans 6:23 says: "For the wages of sin is death; but the gift of God is eternal life through Jesus Christ our Lord."

The scriptures also warn of our failure to recognize sin as a deadly poison. Proverbs 14:12 says: "There is a way which seemeth right unto a man, but the end thereof are the ways of death."

Some years ago, my husband, Charles, mentioned to me the progression of sin that is described in Psalm 1:1 which says: "Blessed is the man that walketh not in the counsel of the ungodly, nor standeth in the way of sinners, nor sitteth in the seat of the scornful." He said, "So many young people and older ones also approach sin in this fashion. First, they begin to walk along beside sin, then they stop and stand: after that it is much easier to pull up a chair and sit and become a part of it." The rest of the Psalm describes the more perfect way.

So what is woman to do? Let's read Matthew 4:1-11. Do you see from this reading the three identifying leaves of temptation?

a. Lust of the eye

b. Lust of the flesh

c. Pride of life.

Do you see the wisdom of Jesus in using three simple words to both identify the sin and protect Himself from the deadliness of it? Those three words are simply:

"It is written."

What a wonderful defense mechanism or insect repellent against sin in its various forms. If we know God's Word, we can say with full assurance: "It is written."

Let me share something interesting with you to challenge your thinking. The "seed" for this book had been planted. In other words, the manuscript was in the hands of the publisher. I had asked the question in it based upon what I have taught and been taught most of my life. I asked "Can you think of a single sin that does not have its roots in one of the categories mentioned above? I cannot."

One day the phone rang and it was my publisher, Tom Estes. He said, "In answer to your question in Chapter IV, I can think of two."

1. Thoughtlessness

2. Those who are sincerely wrong religiously.

Do you agree or disagree? This provides a wonderful thrust for in-depth thinking and open class discussion.

The danger of sin, the identification of sin, our human weakness toward sin, and the protection against or the cure for its ill effects in our lives are clearly revealed in God's Holy Word. Can you and I say, "It is written?"

Sin is like poison ivy. If it appeared unattractive and dangerous, it might not be such a problem. But it often comes attractively packaged and highly advertised. Satan is not idle, nor is He without cunning. He is hard at work to win us over. Use God's word to both identify and resist sin in the rose garden of our heart — there is no other way.

Name some of the ways in which the five areas of sin listed previously show themselves and tempt us today.

a. _____

b. _____

c. _____

d. _____

e. _____

Biblical Examples

I find it gratifying that the Bible gives us examples of both the right and the wrong in the lives of individuals. It shows how we may resist or give in to temptation. This assures me that no one of us is perfect, but, like Paul, we must continue to "press on toward the mark."

Many women tell me that their struggle against materialism is the most difficult temptation they face. It is not a new temptation. It has been around for a long, long time.

Look at Eve: First, she was attracted by the appearance of the forbidden fruit in the garden of Eden (lust of the eye), then she was desirous of knowing how it tasted (lust of the flesh), and when Satan implied that she could be wiser than God, she was caught up in the pride of life. Was thoughtlessness a part of her sin also? How different was her reaction to that of our Lord, who simply said "It is written." Talk about it any way you want to, but the fact remains: Eve sinned because she wanted to do what she wanted to do more than she wanted to do what God wanted her to do. Has the situation changed?

Let's look at materialism as a "lust of the eye" temptation (although it can take many other forms as well).

Look at Abraham. He was very wealthy but he sought to serve God, even though it meant leaving the familiarity and comforts of the life to which he was accustomed. He had his priorities in order. What about his attitude in giving Lot the land which Lot selfishly desired? Abraham knew what was important. His attitude toward God and His desire to do God's will kept him from the temptation of the "lust of the eye" and in terms of "things." Is our problem really materialism or is it priorities?

Look at another biblical example of a different reaction to the temptation of both "lust of the eye" and "pride of life." Read Luke 18:18-23.

The rich young ruler faithfully kept those commandments that were convenient to Him. Yet he lusted for possessions. His possessions possessed Him. He was unwilling to sell them and give to the poor. They were more important to Him than Jesus Christ. It is not "money" or "things" (or lack of them) that create the problem: it is our attitude toward them.

Read Esther Chapter 1. Have someone tell the story of Vashti's deep conviction of her own principles and her courage to stand up for those convictions. What did her courage and her conviction cost her? Discuss what the cost might have been had she obeyed the king's command.

Although we have no record that Vashti was a worshipper of God, her example of resisting the "lust of the flesh" and/or refusing to excite lustful thoughts in the hearts of men is outstanding.

Vashti was not having to control her own lust, but she felt a responsibility to help others control theirs. Do we share her concern for others?

What verse in the Bible refers to our bodies as the temple of God? Is that not a good protection verse for controlling our own lusts and refusing to contribute to the lust of others?

What about biblical examples of the sin of "the pride of life?" Read Genesis, chapters 24-27. Look at what "pride of life" did to change a woman's life. In the space of three chapters we see Rebekah turn from a lovely, loving woman into a woman who prided herself on knowing more than God, so she took matters in her own hands. Could this happen today? Discuss how it could happen and how it could be prevented.

Pride, trusting in her own wisdom, and discontent with God's plan led Rebekah to deceive her husband, influence her son to follow her example and to show favoritism among her children. What was she sharing from the garden of her heart — poison ivy or roses of love? What did it cost her?

Do you think knowing and using the principles found in Proverbs 3:5-7 would have helped her withstand the temptation to take matters in her own hands. Can these few verses strengthen us?

"Trust in the Lord with all thine heart; and lean not unto thine own understanding."

"In all thy ways acknowledge Him, and He shall direct thy paths."

"Be not wise in thine own eyes; Fear the Lord, and depart from evil."

Perhaps there is no better example in all the Bible of resisting temptation of "pride of life" than in the story of Job.

Name some ways Satan used to try to "break Job down."

We can learn from Job that it is not within man to direct His own steps: that God sees the whole picture, while we see only part: and that trials, troubles, temptations and difficulties can make us grow stronger, wiser and more beautiful in the sight of God.

Another outstanding example of resisting pride in our own abilities is found in the words of Joshua, "As for me and my house we will serve the Lord."

Let's Get Practical

How often do we read Biblical examples and think "Oh, things were different then?" Were they really? Few days will pass when each of us will not be tempted as Jesus was. Do we have the knowledge and the courage to use three simple words against our tempters, "It is written?" If not, then you and I have planted poison ivy in our heart's garden and when we share a bouquet from it with family and friends it will be dangerous. It may be poisonous and could be deadly. Can you think of any sin that truly has no effect on any one except the sinner?

For the practical approach to "lust of the eyes," let me share with you *"For Rich Folks"* as written by my friend, Jerrie Barber in the Savannah Newsletter of January 15, 1989.

> *"Command those who are rich in this present age not to trust in uncertain riches, but in the living God, who gives us richly all things to enjoy.*
> *"Let them do good, that they be rich in good works, ready to give, willing to share."* I Timothy 6:17-18.

"I've always been tempted to pass up these verses. Paul was coaching Timothy on how to instruct rich people.

"I once read that someone was rich when they could live on the interest of the interest they had invested. I don't fit into that category, but I read something written by William Boice of Phoenix, Arizona, that has given me more thought on the subject of who's rich."

"Dear Lord,

I have been re-reading the record of the rich young ruler and his obviously wrong choice. But it has set me to thinking. No matter how much wealth he had, he could not: ride in a car; have any surgery; turn on a light; buy penicillin; watch TV; wash dishes in running water; type a letter; mow a lawn; fly in an airplane; sleep on an inner spring mattress; or talk on the phone."

"If he was rich, what am I? In view of my prosperity, I need to obey the commands:

1. Don't be haughty.

2. Don't trust in uncertain riches.

3. Trust in God.

4. Do good.

5. Be rich in good works.

6. Be ready to give.

7. Be willing to share.

"Blessings are promised to those who obey. They will be 'storing up for themselves a good foundation for the time to come that they may lay hold on eternal life' (I Timothy 6:19).

"Riches bring responsibility. Let's use them well."

In all areas of the temptation to go against God's will for our lives, the yielding often begins with only a small thing. If you want to see just how small a thing it takes to come between you and God, try this. Take a penny. Open your Bible to Matthew 6:33 and read the verse thoughtfully. Then put the penny over the word "God" in the verse and you will see just how small a thing can come between you and God and how completely that very small thing can hide Him from your view. But my friend, Mitzi Maynard, pointed out something interesting to me. If we are willing to look carefully, we will see that with the right effort, even money can't come between us and God. Look closely at your penny. Doesn't it say "In God We Trust?"

Let's get practical about "lust of the flesh."

Some of the tools Satan uses to tempt us in this area are: TV, movies, music, books, magazines, and friends, and by promoting the wider acceptance or tolerance of adultery, fornication, immodesty in both men and women, homosexuality, and filthy or suggestive language. The constant influence of these forces is wearing down men and women, boys and girls of all ages. Many of them have been faithful Christians.

A friend of mine, a faithful Christian woman, said to me recently, "I am frightened because I am not as shocked by many evil things as I used to be. I have grown complacent." One is reminded of Alexander Pope's observation: "Evil is a monster of so hideous a face./First, we abhor; then we endure;/then we embrace."

If you want to know if the items listed above can have any effect on our thinking and actions, try this experiment. Take a glass of clear water. Drop in a few drops of cake coloring (any color) and watch it change. That's how subtly the poison ivy of sin in the rose garden of our thoughts can change them from pure white to the darkness of sin.

Another friend of mine had taken in a foster child who came from a home where she had been abused. She was about three years old. She was an obedient child, but she would not eat when the family sat down for a meal. Instead she would sit down and cry. Then later my friend would find her pulling food out of the garbage can and eating it. A check with the social worker revealed that the child had seen her father kill her mother with a butcher knife as they sat at the table. It also revealed that the child had been forced to eat from the garbage can or she would be severely punished. Do you see how quickly, even children, absorb unhealthy attitudes and actions from exposure to poisonous situations.

Discuss some of the current "entertainment" that can cause lustful thoughts and actions? What are some sins to which lust of the flesh can lead?

Discuss what we, as Christian women, can do to reduce the level of unhealthy influence that Satan is thrusting at us, our husbands, and our children today. Because a person is a Christian, does that mean that the poison ivy of temptation cannot grow in her heart's garden? Discuss.

Proverbs 4:23 says "Keep thy heart with all diligence: for out of it are the issues of life."

Would not that be a strong protection against the temptation or lust of the flesh? For the Bible also tells us, "As a man thinketh in his heart so is he."

Read Philippians 4:8 and discuss how few (if any) of the subjects we are instructed to "think on" are a part of the devices Satan uses to tempt us?

We often think of pride of life in terms of doing whatever it takes to gain fame, popularity, prestige or personal glory. Let's look at it from a somewhat different light.

When you are with Christians you have no trouble looking, talking and acting like a Christian. When you are with those who are not Christian, do you have any problems looking, talking and acting like a Christian? Is it not a form of "pride of life" that we feel we must be "one of the crowd?" Is it easier for us to "conform than to be transformed?"

How many times during the past week have you mentioned Christ to anyone? If the answer is "none," why not?

One of my favorite quotations can be a help in overcoming our weakness to be taken in by the crowd we are with (but only if it has meaning to us): "In Christ there is endless hope; without Him a hopeless end."

Do we have the courage to choose the less traveled road?

Poison ivy in our garden is like Satan. It doesn't give up. It fights a hard battle. So we must fight hard and refuse to give up or give in to temptation. Things impossible with man are possible with God.

The most encouraging verse in all the Bible to me as a Christian is Philippians 4:13, "I can do all things through Christ which strengtheneth me."

FOR THOUGHT AND DISCUSSION

1. Which root of poison ivy (lust of the eye, lust of the flesh, pride of life, thoughtlessness or being sincerely wrong religiously) do you consider the most difficult to avoid in today's world? Why?

2. Which is the greater problem today, juvenile delinquency or parental delinquency? Discuss.

3. An interesting activity for a class participation on these topics might be to divide the class into two groups. One will be "devils" and the other "angels." One person is chosen to be "an average Christian." The devils throw (in words) various temptations at her. The angels help her to resist the temptation thrown at her by the devils. But they can only do this by using a related scripture and giving the location of it in the Bible.

4. Discuss how one might as easily share a bouquet of poison ivy from her heart's garden as a bouquet of roses.

5. Share a scripture that is especially meaningful to you in your daily living.

FOR YOUR PERSONAL USE

1. Make a close personal study of the life of Christ. Notice how he handled difficult situations he faced. Make an effort to follow His example.

2. Share a bouquet from your heart's garden this week with someone who needs encouragement or someone who has just come through a difficult time in his or her life.

3. If you know a teen-ager who is in danger of planting poison ivy in her rose garden, share with her some of the things you have learned from this lesson. Let your faith blossom.

MY PRAYER FOR YOU

Dear God, help each of us to realize the depth of thy love and understanding and the power of thy presence in our lives. Help us to lean on thee instead of on our own understanding. Give us wisdom to recognize the poison ivy of sin before it takes over our hearts. Give us courage and wisdom to follow our Lord's example and base our lives (even when we are tempted) upon what is written in thy word. May we never forget that if we know and do thy will, with thy help, we may know the real victory over Satan. In Jesus' name.

Amen

CHAPTER 5

WEEDING AND PRUNING TIME

Introduction:

Ideally one would find space for a rose garden, prepare the soil properly, and plant roses; then sit back and enjoy! It does not happen that way in either the rose garden at our home or in the rose gardens of our hearts. Beautiful roses are produced as a result of constant effort.

Weeds spring up in both, and we often wonder why our flowers do not produce as rapidly as the weeds.

With roses there is also the matter of pruning when the time is right. We must be diligent and observant in both gardens if we are to grow the kinds of roses we desire.

This chapter will look at some weeds that grow in the heart and also at when pruning becomes necessary.

Weeding Our Rose Gardens

No matter how long we have been Christians, nor how new we may be at the Christian walk, weeds do spring up in our hearts. No matter how faithful we may be, the weeds can still push through if we are not aware. The weeds of the heart are many, but we shall discuss only two in this segment — doubt and discouragement. With each we will look first at a Biblical example and then make a practical application.

Read Matthew 14:14-33. Verses 14-21 set the stage, but the weeds of doubt are most evident in the verses 22-33. Could Jesus ask of you and me ". . . O thou of little faith, wherefore didst thou doubt?"

Look at what happened. First, the disciples had seen Jesus take two loaves and five fishes and feed more than 5,000. He had met a very basic need of all mankind - relieving hunger. Yet how quickly his disciples forgot. When the storm arose, they panicked. Then impetuous Peter issued a challenge to the Lord. ". . . Lord, if it be thou, bid me come to thee on the water."

Then we see Jesus meeting another of Peter's needs. He encouraged him to come out on the water. But Peter was filled with doubts at his safety in the storm and cried out for the Lord to save him. Yet, once again, Jesus reached out His hand to meet the need.

How often as we read this account we say, "How could Peter?" Peter could because he was human and because the weeds of doubt can grow both slowly and rapidly in the heart's garden.

The reading ends with those in the ship worshipping Jesus and saying, "Of a truth thou art the Son of God." Yet as we read further in the New Testament about the life of Christ, we see other times when Peter and others doubted. If those who walked with Jesus daily and saw his greatness could doubt so easily, why do we, who cannot see, hear or touch Jesus except through the Word and our obedience to it, feel we are immune to doubts?

Trust in God Removes the Weeds of Doubt

In our own lives doubt or the weeds of doubt grow in our hearts in different forms. Sometimes it is SELF DOUBT which makes us have such a poor opinion of ourselves that we doubt that we have any value or that we could do anything for the cause of Christ. Yet look at Peter. Who would ever have believed that he would preach the first gospel sermon with such success? Acts 4:13 reads, "And when they saw the boldness of Peter and John, and perceived that they were unlearned and ignorant men, they marveled; and they took knowledge of them, that they had been with Jesus." What about you and me? A deep and abiding faith in Jesus enables us to do things we never dreamed possible. I love the little picture of the dejected little boy who says "I know I'm somebody, 'cause God don't make no junk." Let's rid ourselves of that weed of self-doubt so that people will know (as we ourselves know) we have been with Jesus.

Then there is the DOUBT OF OTHERS. We live in a world that does not do a great deal to rid our minds of distrust of others. There are dishonesty, disregard for moral values and for human life on every hand. Fear can rear its ugly head without any problem. There is a better way.

In fact, it is so much better that I suggest each of us memorize the words of the writer of Hebrews in Chapter 13:5-6 and take it as a motto for daily living and for ridding our heart's gardens of weeds:

"Let your conversation be without covetousness; and be content with such things as ye have, for he hath said, I will never leave thee, nor forsake thee.

"So that we may boldly say, The Lord is my helper, and I will not fear what men shall do unto me."

When we put our trust in the Lord, it enables us to feel better about ourselves, enables us to feel more secure from fear, and enables us to seek the good in others. Sometimes finding something good in others and letting them know you appreciate it can keep them from becoming persons we cannot trust.

My daddy used to tell me over and over as I was growing up, "If you will learn to build upon your strengths, then you can minimize your weaknesses. But if you let your weaknesses control your life, then you will never know whether you have any strengths or not."

But if the self-doubt and doubt of others are allowed to grow wild in our heart's gardens then we may find that the next step is to doubt God and His Word. When this happens we often turn away from the things of God and neglect to read His Word, neglect to obey it, and neglect to pray.

Then we become like Peter; we demand signs because we cannot believe that which we cannot see and touch. And when we have turned from God we feel as if there is no one to whom we can cry out. Our lives are filled with questions such as "If God is real, how can he let this happen?" or "Something as old as the writings of the Bible claim to be cannot fit today's needs." How sad! The weeds are choking out the truth and our work becomes harder and harder. We forget to call on God for help.

It doesn't have to be! If only we can remember that Peter's Lord is our Lord, too, then we can put our trust in the Lord. Thereby we remove the weeds of self-doubt, doubt of others, and doubt of the relevancy of God and His Word in the complex world in which we live today.

That does not mean that God will automatically clear the weeds, but He can and will aid us to do so. The calmness of trust in God is the best weed-killer available for the heart of man.

From a church bulletin, the following is attributed to Bobby Bates of Broken Arrow, OK:

"What would you think of one who constantly watered weeds and helped them to grow every way he could, but allowed the flowers to die. Weird! Strange! Demented! However, that is what a lot of us do every day.

"When we continually point out the faults of our loved ones but never compliment them when they do well, we are watering weeds and letting flowers die. A certain amount of constructive criticism is necessary, but a constant diet of it becomes destructive.

"Remember how angry it made you when someone criticized you? It generally did not make you want to improve, did it? However, when someone complimented you, it was encouraging and made you want to do even better, didn't it?

"Your friends and loved ones feel the same way. Don't be hypercritical of them, but make it a habit to look for the good things they do and compliment them. Water the flowers and watch them grow!"

The Weeds of Discouragement

How many times have you ever felt discouraged? Most of us have experienced it at one time or another. It is a weed in our heart's gardens and if allowed to grow untouched can become a cause of despondency, depression, and even destruction. The weed of discouragement allowed to grow in our heart's gardens can cause many diseases which may make us ill or even disable us.

Again, you and I did not invent discouragement. It has been around a long time. In the past, as in the present, different people have handled discouragement in different ways. But there is no record of its having ever been handled successfully without God's help.

The Old Testament gives us the history of Elijah. His difficulties and his discouragement often rivalled a TV mystery for excitement and suspense. Read accounts of his activities in I and II Kings. In I Kings 19 we find that things got so bad for Elijah that he went off into the wilderness and sat under the juniper tree and prayed to die. What happened? Read the rest of the chapter. God met his needs. But even a man of Elijah's stature had given in to discouragement.

Two other Biblical examples that show a different approach to discouraging circumstances are: (1) Read Acts 16:18-40. Try to imagine how discouraging it must have been to Paul and Silas to have been thrown into prison when they were so diligently seeking to serve their Lord. Yet they prayed and sang. God met their needs. They didn't know how or when - but they trusted in the Lord and that gave them the faith to pray and sing, even in the face of insurmountable (so it seemed) difficulties.

Then there is the ultimate example, Jesus Christ. I urge you to read and re-read the life of Christ often. It is an encouraging, thrilling and challenging example to us today. Note how many times Jesus faced great disappointments. Name some of them. Yet Jesus "kept on keeping on." His focus was on Almighty God. Each time I read the words from the cross, "Father, forgive them for they know not what they do," I realize how much we need the attitude of the Christ to propel us into the action God expects of us.

We CAN lean on the Lord in the same way Biblical characters did. God awaits, but God does not force acceptance of the "better way of life" on us; He merely offers it. Doubts and discouragement cloud our sight and our hearing so that we often are unaware of the offer and the security that is found in Christ.

A good memory verse for us in this study would be "And let us not be weary in well doing; for in due season we shall reap, if we faint not." Galatians 6:9.

What lessons can we learn from the three Biblical examples we have just considered? Why is it often difficult to apply these lessons to our daily lives?

Pruning Time

Just as there are many different types of roses, so are each of us different.

Pruning for roses comes at different times and in different ways, depending upon the type of rose. But failure to prune in a timely and proper manner can cause the roses to be less abundant or beautiful than they could have been.

You and I as Christians are much the same. We need pruning in different ways and at different times.

As new Christians we often need pruning early in our Christian walk. We need to prune away false ideas that "now that I am a Christian I will have no problems." The sooner we can realize that the Christian advantage is not the absence of problems in our lives, but the presence of God in our lives, the less pruning will have to be done.

Perhaps there is no better way of sharing roses from the garden of our hearts than by the example we set in handling problems. I am reminded of two women I know. They do not even know each other, yet they are a good illustration of the need for pruning in one life while not in another.

One of these women has faced more problems in her lifetime than I could list. It has been an uphill battle in so many ways, physical, financial, with family problems, and loss of loved ones. Her life has been a steep climb up Heartbreak Hill. Yet she has touched more lives, shared more roses from her garden of love than you would believe. She is strong spiritually, loves to study the Bible and share it with others, and her spiritual sparkle lights the lives of those around her.

By contrast, another woman (who is younger) has faced some minor problems of a physical nature and has given up. She complains constantly and is critical of others because they do not spend their entire time trying to make her happy. She is critical of the church when members do something for her and when they don't. She has a sound financial situation, but refuses to give of herself, her time, her talents or her money. She never shares roses from her heart's garden, but each time she sees you, she, in effect, asks you to walk with her through her garden of thorns, thistles and weeds. She wants you to suffer with her. Oh, how much pruning needs to be done in her life.

Then there is the time in our lives when we become so busy that we have no time for God. How desperately we need to prune the things that keep us from spiritual growth. An interesting test you might wish to take to see if your life is in need of some pruning so that you may have roses to share is this: Make a list of the main things you do in a day's time — the regular and the "sometimes" things. List everything, even eating and sleeping. Then beside each of them list how much time you estimate you spend each day on the activity. Multiply that by 7 and see how you are spending your week. Do you need to prune?

Perhaps one of the most dangerous noxious growths that need to be pruned from our lives is complacency. It can happen to us at any time, and it may require a number of different methods to properly prune it away.

Complacency takes many forms: There is that which leads us to believe we don't need to be concerned about the problems of anyone we do not know. So we just look the other way when we are asked to become involved with taking the gospel to all the world. Certainly not everyone can go in a physical way to faraway places, but each of us can go through prayer and through financial assistance and through encouragement to those who have gone.

Then there is the complacency about the souls of men in general. We feel that by attending every service, participating in the fellowship of the church and by visiting the sick we have done enough. Think about it for a moment, and perhaps you will want to discuss the matter in class. How did you first come to know about becoming a Christian? Who encouraged and influenced you to become a Christian? Now ask yourself — where would I be today if nobody had cared? We must prune complacency in our lives or we'll be unable to share roses from our heart's gardens and we will then share in the responsibility of lost souls. In a college age girls' class I recently asked the question, "Can we wash our hands of those we know who are lost?" One of the students replied, "Pilate washed his hands and Jesus was crucified." Are you and I crucifying Christ afresh by our complacency? Is pruning needed in our lives?

Then there is the matter of self-righteousness. Have we "arrived?" Or, like Paul, must we continue to press on? Do we need to prune the self-righteousness from our lives? I believe there are two tests we may take that will help us to do some much-needed pruning. They are in the scriptures. Look first at II Peter 1:5-11. Read carefully. Before we settle into complacency and/or self-righteousness let's grade ourselves on a 1 to 10 basis (with 10 being the highest). Mark here in your book and then you may wish to discuss generally without revealing how you've graded yourself.

DILIGENCE	1	2	3	4	5	6	7	8	9	10
FAITH	1	2	3	4	5	6	7	8	9	10
VIRTUE	1	2	3	4	5	6	7	8	9	10
KNOWLEDGE	1	2	3	4	5	6	7	8	9	10
TEMPERANCE	1	2	3	4	5	6	7	8	9	10
PATIENCE	1	2	3	4	5	6	7	8	9	10
GODLINESS	1	2	3	4	5	6	7	8	9	10
KINDNESS	1	2	3	4	5	6	7	8	9	10
LOVE	1	2	3	4	5	6	7	8	9	10

Are You Fruitful or Barren?

Now read I Corinthians 13:1-13. List the characteristics of love. What do we need to test ourselves on from this profile of love that is not included in the listing above? Grade yourself in the same manner on those items.

Now that you look at your own personal score, what kind of heart's bouquet is available for you to share with those you meet? Is it sparse and faded? Does it have only a few blossoms? Or is it bright, beautiful and abundant? Your bouquet can be just as beautiful and bountiful as you want it to be. But it takes constant weeding and pruning. It also takes the firm conviction that we can do nothing alone. We need God's help for both weeding and pruning.

As a closing thought, read I Corinthians 3:6-9 and discuss as it applies to this lesson.

FOR THOUGHT AND DISCUSSION

1. What are some weeds and pruning needs that have not been covered in this chapter?

2. What happens in our gardens if we keep putting off weeding and pruning? Is this different from our weeding and pruning in our heart's garden? Why or why not?

3. What is another Biblical example not covered in this chapter that indicates a need for weeding for pruning in the life of an individual in order for that individual to be pleasing to God?

FOR YOUR PERSONAL USE

During the next seven days, with great diligence and with love, put into practice things that will help you to increase the other items listed from II Peter 1.

MY PRAYER FOR YOU

Dear heavenly Father, as I have worked on this book I have often found it painful to face my own weaknesses. I have also found that by using what I write, I am growing spiritually. But most of all, I have realized more than ever before how much it means to me to be a part of YOUR family and to know that I can come to you with things both great and small. How wonderful is the assurance that your grace reaches me.

My prayer is that each person who reads and/or studies this book will find that its purpose is to help us to go to the Bible for instructions in making our heart's gardens what they should be. I pray that we may also know that the size of the garden is unimportant; it is the quality of the blossoms that come from it. Help us, Father, to realize our dependence upon Thee. May we continue to plant and water, weed and prune, but always with the realization that it is YOU who will give the increase.

It is in the name of Jesus Christ that I pray.

Amen

CHAPTER 6

A THING OF BEAUTY IS A JOY FOREVER

Introduction:

On our first wedding anniversary my husband, Charles, was in Italy. It was during the second World War. Mails were slow and often we went through long periods of time without news. I had not heard from him in some time and felt the loneliness more and more as our anniversary date approached. Without my knowing it, far in advance, he had made arrangements with his parents and his sister to purchase and deliver his gift to me. He also had them arrange for the florist to send a dozen red roses on the day of our anniversary. That has been more than 40 years ago. The roses have long since faded and been thrown away. Yet their beauty is as vivid as the day the florist delivered them. The beauty of the thought and love they expressed has been a joy forever.

So it is with the roses we share from the gardens of our hearts. If the bouquet is one of beauty, grown in a pure and loving heart, the joy of that bouquet (whether it is a single bloom or an arm's bouquet) will remain a joy forever.

The purpose of this lesson is to help us to see the beauty and joy that result from what we think, what we say, and what we do. It also has the purpose of helping us to better understand how to keep our thoughts, our words and our actions as beautiful as God has planned for them to be.

THINK ON THESE THINGS

It was Wednesday and I had just written the outline for this chapter and the introduction. I had chosen my scriptures. Then I had to stop and attend worship services. That particular evening a senior Bible major from Freed-Hardeman College, Phillip Brooks, of Columbia, Tennessee, spoke. I could not believe how closely his remarks followed my outline and how much we approached the subject in the same way, despite the differences in our ages. When I mentioned the similarity to my husband, he said, "That's good. Means you are using the same textbook. The time to be concerned is if you were not saying similar things about the same scriptures."

Phillip has given me permission to quote him in this chapter and I hope that when you have studied it, you will say, as a woman said to Phillip, "Hearing this lesson has made me a better person."

Perhaps you have already suspected the scripture that provided the basis for both the sermon and this lesson.

"Finally, brethren, whatsoever things are true, whatsoever things are honest, whatsoever things are just, whatsoever things are lovely, whatsoever things are of good report, if there be any virtue, and if there be any praise, think on these things."   Phil. 4:8

As you think on these things, think what an effect such thoughts have on your words and your actions. Think how much the bouquets you give others from the garden of your heart are colored by the things which fill your mind. Think how thinking on the five things listed in this one verse make you feel better than thinking negatively about things. Think also about how beautiful these thoughts are when we are merely meditating upon them; how much more beautiful they become when by our words they are expressed to others; but how they become a thing of beauty that is a joy forever as they are lived out by the actions of our lives.

Think

How important this five letter word is. As Phillip Brooks pointed out so beautifully in his sermon, everything that IS was first a THOUGHT. God's creation was first thoughts, then words and then action. Man's inventions are the same, but of a human instead of divine nature. Man first has the thought or the idea, then it is put into words in the form of blueprint, detailed layout or whatever is needed. From that is developed by action until it becomes what the original idea had thought it would be.

Yet one of the criticisms we often hear of the world in which we live today is that we do not THINK. We absorb, but we do not think. We allow many things to be poured into our minds without thinking about them. Someone has said, "To live without thinking is to permit good or evil either one to fill our lives. It is to be out of control of our lives. Even if we do no evil, when we live without thinking, we live thoughtlessly. We are out of control and without regard for ourselves, our God and those around us."

When we go to the scriptures to see what is revealed about the heart (mind) we see more clearly how vital it is to our well being. We see, also, how important it is that what we think be the kind of thoughts conducive to godly living. Let's examine some scriptures.

Read Matthew 22:37-40. In the great commandment we learn that God expects us to commit our heart and mind to Him in love. So what we think is important to God.

I Samuel 16:7 helps us to realize something else very important. How often do you and I relate to a person by what we see as outward appearance? But God "looketh on the heart." God not only wants our mind and heart committed to Him, He also knows whether or not it is. Are we willing for God to know our thoughts? If we are fearful or ashamed that God does know what we think, then we need to clean up our act. Proverbs 4:23 tells us "keep thy heart with all diligence." Why?

The Psalms contain beautiful references to the heart. Some of them include: Psalm 27:3 speaks of no fear in the heart; Psalm 28:7 speaks of the trusting heart; Psalm 78:37 reminds us that all hearts are not right with God; Psalm 97:11 shows us there is need for gladness and uprightness of heart; Psalm 119:80 is a prayer for soundness of heart.

Other scriptures refer to the heart as being heavy, able to discern, joyful, prideful, hard, believing, and the list is endless.

As you think about these references to "what we think in our heart," can you not see that the thoughts that come from the heart as God desires can truly be those of beauty and a joy forever?

Proverbs 23:7 tells us that "as we think in our hearts, so are we." Therefore as the writer admonishes in Proverbs 4:23, we should keep our hearts with all diligence. What does that mean?

Now is a time for you and me to stop and THINK seriously. Are we willing to pray with the Psalmist of old "search me and know my heart?"

Speak

Read Luke 6:43-45. These scriptures tells us that it is out of the abundance of the heart that the mouth speaketh. Each time we speak we reveal something that is in our mind and heart.

It is impossible to have a heart and mind filled with beautiful thoughts and speak harsh, ugly, evil things. It is equally impossible to speak beautiful words from a heart and mind filled with evil thoughts. Someone once challenged me on this statement, saying "But hypocrites do not speak what they have in their hearts." My answer is that hypocritical words can never be beautiful words because, in the end, they will always hurt for they are not true.

Think for a moment about all the words you heard during the past week. Which words helped you? Which words hurt you? Think of all the words you said. Were they words that helped or words that hurt?

There are 26 letters in the alphabet, but they wield a powerful force in our lives and in the lives of others. How might we describe some of the words we can speak? Angry, brave, beneficent, cold, caring, concerned, demanding, deceitful, dutiful, depressing, encouraging, evil, eager, edifying, fearful, fair, friendly, foolish, good, godly, grumbling, generous, gracious, grouchy, happy, harmful, helpful, hateful, humorous, humble, intelligent, interesting, indifferent, indecisive, innocent, just, jolly, kind, loving, lascivious, mean, meaningful, nice, not-so-nice, oaths, old-fashioned, pure, perverted, proud, promising, questioning, quiet, reliable, resentful, ribald, reverent, silly, sensible, sullen, sunny, truths, tirades, unhappy, useful, vicious, victorious, wise, welcome, wicked, yielding, zealous. Which words would make a more beautiful heart's bouquet? Perhaps as a class you will wish to choose some of the types of words (or add others) and discuss them as to the influence they have.

Act

The power of thought is overwhelming. It governs our attitudes, our words, and our actions. Proverbs 23:7 warns us that we are what we think. Then how carefully we should guard our thoughts.

Once again the Apostle Paul comes to mind as an example. As Saul, his heart was filled with bitterness and hatred and his actions revealed those thoughts. I think of the time when Stephen was stoned and according to verse 58 of Acts 7, "and cast him out of the city, and stoned him; and the witnesses laid down their clothes at a young man's feet, whose name was Saul." There is no record in this account of Saul actually saying or doing anything. Yet by his silence and inaction, he revealed what was in his heart and mind. So we sometimes, by our silence and inactivity, do as Saul and "hold the coats" of those who do and so speak evil? I think we do.

Can you think of some examples where by our silence we are encouraging or condoning evil? Can you think of some examples where it would better to keep silent at the moment than to stir up strife?

Now let's look at the change when Saul became Paul. He truly became a new creature and not only was his name changed, but also his thoughts, his words, his actions. That is what happens to us when we are baptized into Christ. We become a new creature. First our hearts and minds are changed and then our words and actions. The account of the changes in Paul's life is an exciting story. But it is no more exciting than the changes in an individual's life when he or she becomes a Christian.

Do we, all too often, tend to put more emphasis on "doing" than on "being." Both are important, but until we become a heart and mind what God wants us to be, it will not matter how much we "do," it will have no lasting effect. Doing without being reminds me of an artificial rose I sometimes use in teaching. It is so beautiful. At a distance you would not be sure if it were real or artificial. It even feels real. I can spray it with a rose-scented perfume and it even smells real. But the fact remains that it is nothing more than an artificial rose. So it is when our words and actions do not come from hearts and minds filled with love for God and man. They are nothing more than artificial.

How do we do it?

A young teenage friend of mine said, "I know what I should do but I don't know how to get myself to do it." Most of us face this same problem at different times in our lives. What can be done? Let's go back and re-read Philippians 4:8. What are we to think on — things true, honest, just, pure, lovely and of good report.

True

When I read things written by men or women, I may not know whether or not they are true. Remember the writer who wrote such a convincing "made up" account that she was considered for a Pulitzer Prize. . . but was it all false? Each time I pick up my Bible I feel so grateful. I know that it is true. I believe what it teaches. I believe that grass and flower may wither and fade, but the Word of God will stand forever. What a feeling of confidence that gives me. So for thinking of things that are true we can confidently go to the Bible for the principles of truth itself.

If we fill our minds with filth, perversion, violence, and deceit, how can truth survive? If we listen to (and often repeat) rumor and gossip, how can truth survive in our hearts and minds? Perhaps we need to learn the child's song that warns to "be careful, little eyes, what you see; ears, what you hear; lips, what you say; hands, what you do and feet, where you walk." We do not think on truth by always thinking on things that oppose truth or things that are not true. Reading our Bible and praying are two ways to think on things that are true. Meditating is another way. Sit for a moment and meditate on a great truth we can share with someone else. Share in class some ideas.

If we were picking a bouquet from our garden, we'd pick our most beautiful roses and blend them into a colorful and harmonious bouquet. So it is with our heart's bouquet. We will want to add some other things to whatsoever things are true.

Honest

This is closely related to what is true. Yet so often a "little dishonesty" seems to be acceptable in the society in which we live. Have you ever taken the test that asks "Am I totally honest?" It is very simple. It requires only yes or no answers, but it calls for some serious soul searching. Here are some of the questions.

1. Have I ever slipped around from my parents?

2. Have I ever lied when I was caught doing wrong?

3. Have I taken things from my employer that belonged to him?

4. Have I been dishonest with him in not giving him an honest day's work for an honest day's pay?

5. Have I ever cheated on my spouse?
6. Have I ever padded an expense account?
7. Have I lied about my child's age to let them in to something at a reduced rate?
8. Have I ever cheated on a test?
9. Have I ever offered God an excuse for not serving Him, rather than a reason?
10. Have I ever kept the change when I received too much back?

Honesty adds much radiance to the heart's bouquet, but it also often takes a great deal of courage for us to be honest with ourselves. Yet without basic honesty we have no complete bouquet to share.

Just

Isn't it wonderful that God's grace permits Him to give us what we need and not what we deserve? That is mercy at its highest level. Would that we as humans beings could so easily be just and merciful to one another. We talk a lot about "double standards" but perhaps the double standard is more clearly seen when we use one standard for measuring our own conduct, expecting justice and mercy, and quite another one for the other fellow. A very cynical friend of mine (not a Christian) says that "with money a person can buy his own justice." I agree that money has often colored court decisions and promotions or honors. But I question seriously that any justice, promotion or honor gained by the exchange of money has any lasting quality. I know it has no eternal values. If we cannot forgive, can we ever be just in our words, our thoughts and our actions? How many times have you ever thought (or perhaps even said), "Well, I hope they get what's coming to them?" Is that being just? Discuss.

Lovely

Our world is filled with the ugly and the lovely. It is filled with darkness and light. We choose what we see. Nothing is more depressing than someone who sees only what's wrong. It is like the woman who goes to a beautiful party and remembers "the glass I had had a chip in it." Or the envious young lady who points out to everyone the spot on a rival's lovely dress. Those are material things, but what about when we try to use a perfection measuring stick for our brothers and sisters in Christ? Learn to think about lovely things. As we look for the lovely, people and things become more lovely.

As I have taught ladies' classes, I have sometimes asked that members of the class bring something to class that they considered "lovely." Some have brought a child's picture, a perfect rose, a picture of a sunset, a meaningful Bible verse, a beautiful poem, a note of encouragement they had received. What would you bring? Of all the lovely things of which I can think, the love of God and Christ for mankind is by far the most lovely. It is boundless and without limitations. How difficult for us to realize that God does not want anyone to be lost and that God and Christ can love us completely, even though we have sinned to such an extent that we have separated ourselves from them. Theirs is a love that is "in spite of" and not "because of." What can be more lovely?

"Of good report" — do we focus on things of good report in our own lives and in the lives of others? Our political system shows us how frequently people are willing to go to any lengths to get the "dirt" on someone else and then "spill it." When you hear of the good that someone has accomplished, do you tell it as eagerly as you do something that is not of good report?

We have seen some examples in recent years of Christians who were talking one way and living another. If they are in public eye, there is much publicity and it becomes a dinner table topic in many households. Would we talk as eagerly about the influence of a Christian of "good report."

What about our lives? If someone were to describe us to a stranger, what would he say? Would he have anything good to report? Do we speak those things which are true? Do we seek to know God's Truth? Are we honest in all things - even when no one is looking? Are we just or unjust? Do we say, do, think and reflect lovely things? Is our life such that the non-Christian would want to be like us?

Think on these things - if the answer to all those questions above is "yes" then our lives will be a thing of beauty and a joy forever. Because we are not perfect, there will be times when we fail, but the beauty of God's love for us is found in his willingness to forgive.

Once again, I ask you to meditate on the life of Christ. What a beautiful life — truth, honesty, purity, justice, loveliness and good report — all found in abundance in one single life that changed the world.

FOR THOUGHT AND DISCUSSION

Choose a Bible character who represents each of the six things upon which we are asked to think — truth, honesty, purity, justice, things that are lovely, things of good report. Discuss.

FOR YOUR PERSONAL USE

During the next week make it a point to allot some time to meditate on God's Word as it relates to this lesson.

Then do at least one thing in each category during the week: Share the Truth with someone, refuse to listen to a lie or a rumor; be honest, even with yourself, try to show justice and mercy in a difficult situation, share something lovely with another, do something that God would consider of "good report" without seeking personal recognition for it. What a colorful and radiant bouquet you will share with others from your heart if you do this.

MY PRAYER FOR YOU

Dear Father, please help each of us to learn the value of eternal things. Help us to know that our salvation made possible by our response to Christ's death on the cross for our sins, is a thing of beauty and a joy forever.

Help us to live in such a way that Christ will be reflected even in a dark world. Help us to do more than just read, that we are to think about things that are true, honest, just, lovely and of good report. Help us also to practice those things in our daily lives that we may share them with others.

We are so grateful for your love, Father. We love You so much, Father. May all that we think, say, and do, be "of good report" in Your eyes.

May we always know the beauty and the joy that is to be found in the Christian way of life.

In Jesus' name we pray.

Amen

PART II

BLOOM WHERE YOU'RE PLANTED

BLOOM WHERE YOU'RE PLANTED

You never ask for a place in the sun,
　　Nor do you try to hide from rain,
You "bloom" upon the mountain tops of joy
　　But also in the vales of pain.

You bloom "wherever you are planted,"
　　And the world becomes a better place
Because of the kind of life you live
　　And the smile upon your face.

Whenever there is work to do
　　You always do your part.
You ever have a prayer and word
　　For those with heavy heart.

You never seek the praise of men.
　　You simply do your Father's will.
You never flaunt your Christian life,
　　You merely try to make it REAL.

You "blossom" in so many, many ways
　　We often take your "bloom" for granted,
But we're pausing now to try to say,
　　"Thanks for blooming where you're planted."

　　　　　　　　　Louise Barnett Cox

CHAPTER 7

BLOOM WHERE YOU ARE PLANTED
AS A SINGLE PERSON

Introduction:

Think of the most beautiful rose garden you have ever seen. In it you found many different types of roses and many different colors. They blended together to make a beautiful scene. No one would have said, "That rose is white, while all the others are brightly colored. So it doesn't belong."

Yet, are we not guilty of "categorizing" people? Look at the group known as "singles." We, and they, often tend to set them apart as not blending well with those in other categories. Isn't that foolish? Singles come in different sizes, colors, ages, situations, abilities, and attitudes, just as people in other categories do. They are a part of God's family and they possess a distinct beauty that is all its own.

This lesson is written as a challenge to those who are single and to those who are not. It is a challenge for each of us to see our worth as God's creation and our value in God's plan for His family. It is a challenge to "bloom where you are planted" (no matter what the circumstances), for it takes each one of us blended together to make the beautiful, colorful heart's bouquet that God intends us to be. Yet at the same time, it is possible for a single rose from the garden of one's heart to be the most significant bouquet ever shared with another.

What is your status in life — single? Perhaps you have never married. Perhaps you are widowed. Perhaps you are divorced. The point is that you are the only person who is currently a part of your intimate lifestyle. You may live alone, or you may live with children, parents, or share a home with another single friend.

While this may be the lifestyle SOME have chosen, the chances are very good that it is not what you have chosen. Yet this is where you find yourself. How do you face it?

Can you see the value in one life well-lived, no matter the circumstances? Although we are all, in a sense, dependent upon others (and certainly upon God), can you see your lifestyle as complete and rewarding, even if you are not an appendage to another person?

I would be the first to say that to be happily married and have children would be the ideal situation for most of us. But it is not the only way.

Are you blooming where you are planted? Or are you withdrawing and refusing to be a part of society because you may not feel your present status is acceptable?

Instead of thinking of what you would do if you were in a different lifestyle, list three things you can do to make your present lifestyle more meaningful. If you are not single, list three things you think of that might help a single live a more meaningful life.

1. _____

_____

2. _____

_____

3. _____

_____

Ask yourself, "Am I blooming where I'm planted, or am I withering away because I am not happy with my circumstances?"

May I suggest something that will help each of us (whatever our status) to bloom more profusely?

> *God, grant me the serenity to accept*
> *the things I cannot change:*
> *The courage to change the things I can,*
> *And the wisdom to know the difference.*

May each of us learn to say with the Apostle Paul ". . . for I have learned in whatsoever state I am, therewith to be content." (Philippians 4:11)

Looking Back to Biblical Characters

As I prepared this lesson, I was fascinated by the number of Biblical characters (both men and women) who give us great examples for living and yet no mention whatever is made of their marital status. That tells me something very important that I believe we all often forget: Until we first see ourselves as Christian women, we cannot bloom where we are planted. Being a Christian woman is more important to God — and to me — than any other role I will ever fill. I do not have to be married to be a Christian woman. Think about this. It doesn't matter if I am single, widowed, married, with or without children; unless I am first of all a Christian woman, my life is empty and meaningless in the long term aspects.

The two best examples of the value of a **single life** found in the Bible are, of course, Jesus and Paul. They lived lives of love for God, sacrifice, service, and fulfillment, even in the most difficult circumstances. No one could ever accuse either of them of refusing to "bloom where they were planted."

But let's look at some women. They showed us how effective they could be: Dorcas, Lydia, Ruth, Naomi, and Anna.

No mention is made of Dorcas' family, but look at the difference she made in the lives of others. (Have someone tell of Dorcas' work). Would you say that she shared a heart's bouquet? Here was a woman who made a difference in the lives of others. What greater way to bloom where one is planted and to share our heart's bouquet?

Then look at Lydia. Although her "household" is mentioned, many commentators seem to think that referred to her household staff. We do know that she worked outside the home, but did not let that interfere with her religious interests. In an age such as we live in today, where women are falling all over themselves to gain recognition as "a first" in some area, Lydia stands out. How many of us would be willing to be the first convert in the U.S., or even in our own state, our own country, or our own town? She is an outstanding example of the value of "one life" and the impact of a single rose shared from a heart's bouquet. Not only did Lydia wield an influence for Christianity while she lived, but how many times is she used to encourage those in the world today to have the courage to "bloom where they are planted."

Then there is Ruth; she had a heartache, but it did not make her close her eyes and her feelings for others. When Naomi was going back to her own people alone, Ruth made her choice and said those oft-quoted words, ". . . thy people shall be my people and thy God shall be my God." Read the story of Ruth and Naomi and discuss it from the standpoint of two widows' handling of the loss of their husbands.

And then there is Anna; the Biblical account speaks for itself as far as the impact of one "blooming where she is planted" is concerned. The King James account in Luke 2:36-39 reads as follows:

"And there was one Anna, a prophetess, the daughter of Phanuel, of the tribe of Aser; she was of a great age, and had lived with a husband seven years from her virginity;

"And she was a widow of about fourscore and four years, which departed not from the temple, but served God with fastings and prayers night and day.

"And she coming in that instant gave thanks likewise unto the Lord, and spake of him to all them that looked for redemption in Jerusalem.

And when they had performed all things according to the law of the Lord, they returned into Galilee, to their own city Nazareth."

What were the circumstances surrounding this account? Discuss how Anna "bloomed where she was planted" despite being a widow and despite her age.

A Look at Women Today

As I talked with a number of women who fall into the "singles" category, I asked them to tell me some of the problem areas that they faced. Here are the ones that recurred most frequently:

(a) Fighting the constant feeling of rejection or failure.

(b) Not feeling accepted into other groups.

(c) Loneliness.

(d) Needing someone with whom they could talk confidentially.

(e) Resentment at being teased about never having married or being asked the question, "What's a good-looking gal like you doing not married?"

(f) Not finding fulfilling areas for involvement in the church.

(g) Divorcees said their feeling of being rejected was their most severe problem.

(h) Widows listed "loneliness" as their major problem.

(i) Those who had never married often question whether they have set their standards too high.

Would you add any to this list? How can one cope with these feelings? One has but to look around and see that different women handle the situation differently. Some withdraw and refuse to cope; others develop a defiant and angry attitude that colors all they do. Still others become desperate and are willing to settle for something second rate. Yet there are many who live rich, full, rewarding lives. They are those who share generously with others the blossoms from their heart's gardens.

These are some examples that come from people I know. Their names have been changed and some of the circumstances so as not to reveal their true identity, but their examples will be clear.

Annie Anxious

Annie is a college student. She is a fine young Christian woman whose chief desire is to be a wife and mother. She has very high ideals and expectations. She is a popular young lady and has dated a number of different young men. Yet one night as we talked in a very serious vein, she asked, "Should I lower my standards? Do you think I am too picky?" Of course, I insisted that she maintain high standards for herself and for the man she would be willing to marry. I explained that such standards might reduce her options, but that the final result would be worth the waiting. We talked of God's standards for those whom He had created. We talked of the need for patience in all aspects of our lives. Time passed. One night I received a call. Annie cried as she told me how much she appreciated my encouragement. She had met, dated, and was going to marry a fine young man whose standards, if anything, were even higher than hers. She said, "The waiting was not easy, but it was worth it."

Alice Available

I learned about Alice from some young men who know her. She is attractive, has a good personality, and is fun to be with. As one fellow said, "a truly nice girl." Then what's her problem? As one of the young men said, "She is so **available**." She is afraid that she won't have a date and that she won't get married that she takes the lead. As one young man said, "It is as if she is wearing a sign that says 'Hey, look, fellows, I'm available.' You are afraid to ask her for a date for fear she will take it as a proposal for marriage." Whatever else Alice is, she is insecure as an individual and feels she must have a companion. Yet as an individual, she has much more to offer than many of her girl friends who have dates, or are already happily married. It is just that she is over-eager.

Kathy Content

Kathy is older, but still unmarried. She would like to be happily married, but she is content with life as it is until "Mr. Right" comes along. She is successful in her career, has a number of good friends of both sexes, enjoys many different types of activities, and is very involved in the work of the church. But perhaps her secret lies in the fact that she is always doing something for someone else, big things, middle-sized things, little things, whatever she sees as a need. She is too busy to be wrapped up in herself.

Betty Bitters

Betty had a good marriage, but her husband died suddenly, and she become a bitter old woman overnight. She has isolated herself from everyone. Talk with her and you'd think she was the only person in the world who ever lost a husband. Nothing pleases her. She is bitter towards God and toward family, friends, and even strangers. She is in excellent health and has no financial worries, but she refuses to see that she has any blessings. She does not attend church and says she has quit praying. Her attitude and actions have had a negative effect on her parents and her children.

Emily Encourager

What a contrast Emily is. A striking looking woman and a good woman, it appeared she had everything going for her. Then one day, without warning, her husband walked out and left her for a younger woman. He left her with no marketable skills of her own and with two small children. She was stunned and she was crushed. As she talks with me about it, she says, "After about a week of total numbness, I realized that I had to pick up the pieces. I realized that I could not pick them up alone, so I turned to God. I prayed for wisdom and for an attitude that would not leave me bitter. I prayed also that I would never talk with my children against their father. It was difficult for them and I determined to make it as easy as possible."

Emily took special training and obtained a good job in a local bank. She continued faithfully serving the Lord in many ways. But the greatest thing she did for others, for herself, and for her children was her "encouragement." She found little ways — notes, words, phone calls, prayers, services — to encourage people of all ages and taught her children to do the same. She says, "I have never encouraged anyone is any way, that I have not been more encouraged myself. The hurt is still there. I hope that when I meet someone else, I will not be afraid to try again. There are many wonderful men in the world and perhaps someday I shall meet and marry one of them."

There are many other examples, but time does not permit. Think about the attitudes and actions of each of these examples given, and remember that one does not have to be a single to be like these women — it could happen to any of us.

But What's a Woman to do?

Let's look at the role of the "single" from two perspectives: (1) from her own perspective and (2) from the perspective of "others" in her life.

(1) **What's a single woman to do?**

a. Put her trust in God. Remember God sees the whole picture. Ours is but a limited view.

b. Count your blessings. You probably know someone who lives in your own town whose married life is a disaster. Would you change places?

c. See yourself as an individual. God does. You are of value or God would not have planned so well for you, nor would Christ have died for you. You do not need anyone else in order to claim God's blessings.

d. Open your eyes. Look at your opportunities. You probably have a job that puts you in touch with others. Use that opportunity to be an influence for Christ. Use it as opportunity to learn new things and meet new people. Refuse to live in a space too small for a rose garden.

e. Reach out to others. Don't sit and feel sorry for yourself. Reach out to others — those who need you and those who don't. Project a positive attitude.

f. Open your home. Invite others into your home (and your life). Refuse to become a "couch potato" no matter how much you may want to.

g. Pray. Pray sincerely. Pray, believing. Pray fervently. Realize that God's wisdom exceeds yours, so His answer may surprise you, but it will be superior to all you could ever ask. Pray with thanksgiving.

h. Develop strong Christian friendships.

i. Volunteer. If there is something you can do, don't wait to be asked. Offer. Use your talents.

j. As you develop each of these actions and attitudes in your life (along with patience), you are becoming even more special. Never sell yourself short.

k. Never forget the old quotation, "The best angle from which to approach any problem is the try-angle."

(2) What can others do?

a. Refuse to categorize people in groups, but see them as individuals.

b. Offer your friendship with no strings attached.

c. Encourage others to become involved in service.

d. Never hesitate to talk with others about Christ.

e. Practice what you preach.

f. If you are married, invite those who are not to enjoy activities with you and other couples.

g. Suggest Bible study classes that approach "the whole woman", not mere "singles", "wives", and "mothers."

h. Watch your tongue. Do not pry into personal matters. Do not repeat confidences. Do not tease or joke about any person's status.

i. Do not assume that because a woman is not married, she has all the time in the world. Single women have their jobs, housekeeping, and many other chores. Do not expect them to carry more than their share of the load in "service."

j. Encourage by sharing bouquets from your garden of love.

k. Practice Matthew 7:12 in all your relationships with others.

FOR THOUGHT AND DISCUSSION

Divide the class into small groups. If possible, include those who are single and those who are not in each of the groups. Select a spokesperson for each group. Discuss the role of the single in:

1. The church

2. The home

3. The community

Have each group report on ideas, suggestions, problems, and solutions.

FOR YOUR PERSONAL USE

List the qualities of your life that you feel are pleasing to God. Ask yourself if those qualities don't make you a better person in human relationships also.

List the qualities in your life that may be stumbling blocks to you and others. What can you do to rid yourself of the undesirable qualities?

Do something for someone else each day. Pray for someone else.

MY PRAYER FOR YOU

Dear loving, heavenly Father. Help those who are single by reason of either choice or circumstances to realize that they are not unloved. Help them, Father, to know the depths of Your love for them and that You are no respecter of persons.

But help me also, Father. Help me to be more understanding and to reach out in love. Help me not to see people in categories, but as individuals.

May those who are single learn to love You, themselves and others, for without love we will all be but clanging noise.

May each of us be strength, encouragement and edification one to the other, and may all men know that we are disciples of Christ as we show love one to another. In Jesus' name.

Amen

CHAPTER 8

BLOOM WHERE YOU'RE PLANTED AS A WIFE

Introduction:

"And the Lord God said, It is not good that the man should be alone, I will make him an help meet for him." (Genesis 2:18)

With those words God gave woman one of the greatest privileges and challenges the world has to offer. He also gave purpose to her very existence. Yet those of us who may read this book today have seen a change in attitude toward this role take place in the world. It was gradual at first. Then it became more widespread. Finally, the negative attitude toward woman's role as God planned it has become overwhelming. Divorce rates climb. Marriage problems mount. Women feel called upon to apologize for being homemakers.

The purpose of this lesson is to try to help us to discover the wife's role as God planned it in all its splendor, opportunity, privilege, responsibility and magnitude. It is to challenge each of us to "bloom where we are planted" and that we may encourage others to do so, regardless of the circumstances in which we may find ourselves.

I feel more qualified to write this chapter of "HEART'S BOUQUET" than any other. Why? Because I will soon celebrate 47 years of a very happy marriage to the same man. I am grateful to God for the plan, the purpose, and the joy that is mine to enjoy because of the wisdom of His plan. It was William Law who wrote long, long ago this statement which helps us to see that God is with us in our marriages if only we are willing:

"A root set in the finest soil, in the best climate, and blessed with all that sun and air and rain can do for it, is not in so sure a way of its growth to perfection, as every man may be whose spirit aspires after all that God is ready and infinitely desirous to give him. For the sun meets not the springing bud that stretches toward him with half that certainty as God, the source of all good, communicates Himself to the soul that longs to partake of Him."

When we take God into our marriage partnership, then it will be much easier for us to "bloom where we are planted as a wife."

Planting for Abundant Bloom

As we've talked about before, if we want a rose garden, we will not plant some other type flowers. So it is with marriage. If we want a marriage that is pleasing to God, then we cannot try to build it by standards other than those given us by God.

It reminds me of cooking. My mother was a "pinch of this and a pinch of that" cook. So as a beginning cook, it was very difficult for me to learn to cook as well as she did. God's recipe for a happy marriage is not like that. It is simple, clear, and explicit. He makes no promise for a marriage without its ups and downs, but there is promise for "grace sufficient for all our needs." So perhaps the first thing we need to do is to look at what the Bible says about this role of wife.

Genesis 2:18

> *"And the Lord God said, It is not good that the man should be alone; I will make him an help meet for him."*

This gives us purpose and it defines a specific role that God has in mind for us to fill. "A suitable help." What does that mean to you? To me, as far as my marriage is concerned, it has always meant that I am to be willing to be a suitable help to my husband to enable him to be all that God wants him to be. But I believe also that in doing this, I have opportunity to be all that God wants me to be. I fail to see anything inferior, narrow, or degrading about this role. In fact, at times, it seems overwhelming.

The "help" my husband needs may not be the help another husband needs, but all husbands (and wives) need help to reach the goal of Heaven when life on earth is over.

Discuss some ways in which a wife may help her husband. Discuss ways in which she may hinder a husband. Analyze both lists and determine which would contribute more to the happiness of both marriage partners, helps or hindrances.

But let's look at some other verses.

"A virtuous woman is a crown to her husband; but she that maketh ashamed is as rottenness in his bones."

Virtue may be construed in two ways in the marriage relationship — sexual purity and courage. With more and more women entering the workforce and the general attitude toward sexual promiscuity becoming more and more lax, this probably is more of a problem today than when our parents were first married. Yet the existing situations do not change God's attitude toward sexual purity within and without the marriage boundaries, and it should not change ours.

Hebrews 13:4, states, "Marriage is honorable; let us all keep it so, and the marriage bond inviolate; for God's judgment will fall on fornicators and adulterers." Ephesians 5 states that husbands should love their wives as Christ loved the church and that ". . . In the same way men also are bound to love their wives, as they love their own bodies. In loving his wife a man loves himself."

God has given rather explicit guidelines for the sexual relatonship in marriage. In I Corinthians 7:1, Paul begins instructions for husband and wife to conduct themselves so that they might not "be tempted by Satan." In the New English Version, it reads:

". . . because there is much immorality, let each man have his own wife and each woman her own husband. The husband must give his wife what is due to her, and the wife equally must give the husband his due. The wife cannot claim her body as her own; it is her husband's. Equally the husband cannot claim his body as his own; it is his wife's. Do not deny yourselves to one another, except when you agree to a temporary abstinence in order to devote yourselves to prayer; afterwards you come together again; otherwise, for lack of self control, you may be tempted by Satan."

Any woman who would use the sexual relationship to manipulate her husband is beneath contempt and vice versa. Nor should husbands and wives make unrealistic or over romantic demands on each other, but should realize that a loving, unselfish sexual relationship affects all aspects of the marriage and helps maintain sexual purity for both.

A woman has the right to expect sexual purity from a husband as much as he does from her. "Trust" is a vital ingredient in any marriage, and trust cannot exist when one must always wonder about the sexual faithfulness of a mate. Trust in God and the instructions he has given for marriage is the best fortification against both fornication and adultery.

A man needs courage from the woman he marries. This may take many forms; it may be the courage to help him change the direction of his life when it is headed toward disaster; it may be the willingness to do as Sarah did and leave the comfortable and familiar for a location that is not well known. It may be the courage to stand for the right when everyone else among one's friends is unwilling to do so. A man of courage is made more courageous when he has the courageous support of his wife.

We are all familiar with the value of a virtuous woman; "her price is far above rubies."

Proverbs 14:1

"Every wise woman buildeth her house; but the foolish plucketh it down with her hands."

Perhaps one of the easiest ways to "pluck it down" is by constant nagging. (Find scriptures that relate to nagging.) How much more wonderful a marriage would be if the wife (and the husband) would learn to use the blossoms from the heart's bouquet found in I Corinthians 13 to share their love each day instead of continually nagging. (Discuss how I Corinthians 13 may be used to strengthen a marriage and help a wife to bloom where she is planted.) Do you feel happier when you've shared something positive or when you have nagged?

Proverbs 19:14

". . . A prudent wife is from the Lord."

Using the word prudent to apply to our money management skills probably touches each of us. There are so many things to buy, advertisements make them so attractive, and credit cards make buying so temporarily easy that it is said, "America's love affair with living on credit may be credited with much of its falling out of love in families."

Discuss why being able to manage family finances well would make a wife a "suitable help for her husband." If you have money management ideas that have helped you, share them with the class.

I once heard a speaker say, "The three main bugaboos of marriage are the bedroom, the budget and boredom." Do you agree or disagree? If God is a part of our marriage, wouldn't we be better able to handle any of the three because we played by His rules and not the rules of the world? (Discuss).

Mark 10:6-9

"... from the beginning of the creation God made them male and female. For this cause shall a man leave his father and mother and cleave to his wife; and they twain shall be one flesh; so then they are no more twain, but one flesh. What therefore God hath joined together, let no man put asunder."

If you and I can understand, accept, and apply this one verse, it will be a great help to us in "blooming where we are planted as a wife."

The first four words in the book of Genesis give us a starting point for blooming where we are planted in any role or circumstance we may find ourselves. It says simply "In the beginning God." When God is at the beginning of our plans, our thoughts, our attitude, and our action, we can know we are on the right track. But on to the verses in Mark 10. "God made them male and female." Here are two vital points for blooming where we are planted as a wife. (1) We are God's creation and we should conduct ourselves as godly women, not women of the world. (2) God made us different from men and we should be grateful for the difference and respect it. Our differences should not alienate us one from another, but instead should enable us to complement one another. Each of us is more complete ourselves because of the differences supplied by the mate of the opposite sex.

A simple example of this is found in my own marriage. I am not good with numbers. But Charles is a former Math teacher. So he can handle those things I struggle with, and we both look good. He has great ideas, but words do not come easily for him. So I can help him with learning to express himself more clearly, and we both profit from improved communication skills. The differences God made between man and woman go much deeper than that, but they are not to be scorned or ignored; they are to be appreciated.

"For this cause shall a man leave his father and mother and cleave to his wife." I believe this applies to wives as well as husbands. Think of the powerful message here and the great wisdom. If you and I are not ready to "cut the apron strings," then we are not mature enough for marriage. As parents we need to encourage married children to learn to stand on their own feet. Surely we should be there for them, but never should we become a crutch that would prevent them from cleaving to one another.

Perhaps the greatest secret to "blooming where you are planted as a wife" is found in the words, "and they twain shall be one flesh." Marriage should make us one. We are no longer separate individuals pulling in opposite directions, nor even two people going in the same direction. Instead we are so much a part of one another that we feel one another's joy and pain without words being spoken. Our greatest happiness comes from seeing the greatest happiness in our mate. This is not always easy, for we are basically selfish. We want our own way. "Submission" has become a scorned and hated word. Yet when it is achieved in a marriage or in our relation to Christ, it provides a setting that gives both parties joy, peace, love, understanding and encouragement. There is nothing in the word "submission" to indicate slavery. It simply means that we become one flesh, and, when that happens, we become unaware of the fact that we have also become submissive to someone who loves us even more than we love ourselves. So, you say, your husband is not meeting his role as God would have him do. Does that relieve you of your responsibility to live by God's rules instead of your own? Or does it relieve you of the challenge to "bloom where you are planted as a wife?" I think not. Many a man has been changed by the behavior and conversation of his wife, either for good or for bad.

And how clearly stated is the phrase "what God hath joined together, let no man put asunder." If you were to check the laws of the area in which you live, you would find numerous reasons that could be used for obtaining a divorce. All the laws in the land cannot and will not change God's Word. But you and I have to make choices as to which we will believe.

If we marry for love and to fulfill the role God planned for us, it is much easier to bloom where we are planted than if we marry for other reasons. Here are some reasons people give for marrying today. (Discuss and see if you can add others.)

1. Convenience
2. To get away from home.
3. Because I am bored.
4. So I can have my own freedom.
5. To give a father to my child conceived out of wedlock.
6. Because it is expected that women in our family marry.
7. To keep from having to go to school.
8. With his income and mine we can live better.
9. I feel sorry for him.
10. He is from a prominent family. It will give me social status I have never enjoyed.

What problems can you see arising from a marriage entered into for any of these reasons?

Marriage Insurance Policies

We live in a world where "insurance" has become a necessity to prevent being wiped out by suits filed against us by selfish, greedy people. Think about the following "insurance policies" as tools for preventing either husband or wife from seeking a divorce:

1. Making a real commitment to marriage.
2. Making God the third person in your marriage triangle.
3. Seeking the other's happiness more than you seek your own.
4. Look more at "being" in terms of your own life and his than you look at "doing."
5. Marry a Christian.
6. Learn to forgive.
7. Continue to grow spiritually.
8. Learn to measure success by God's standards and not those of the world.
9. Remember that love and submission are not opposite forces pulling against each other, but two strengthening forces pulling in the same direction.
10. Read the book of James and see how many things you find in the reading that will help you to bloom where you are planted as a wife, if you are willing to be "a doer of the Word and not a hearer only."

From My Marriage Diary

No two marriages will be exactly alike, for no two people are alike. God's plan for marriage does not change, but the ways in which we accomplish that plan may be varied in each marriage. Because I know more about my own marriage than any other, I am going to give you a glimpse into what might well be called my "Marriage Diary."

First, before we married, Charles told me two things that were important to him. One was that it was more important to him that I spend time with him and go with him if he needed to travel than it was to have a spotless house and seven course meals. Second, he was very insistent on the fact that we should not have "double standards." He didn't mean what we usually think of in that term; instead he meant that we wouldn't put on "company manners." We would live so that company would be welcome at any time. He said, "I am as good as anyone who will come to visit, so I don't want us saving dishes, linens, manners for a time when company comes. I want us to be as polite and considerate of each other all the time as we would be of a guest in our home." That has certainly made it easier for me to bloom where I am planted.

Another thing that is important to both of us is how we begin the day. (I realize this is our way; yours may be different). We get up an hour earlier each day in order to have time to have a devotional together, talk a bit and plan our day. Our breakfast room table is in front of our patio doors and to sit there and sip coffee, study, pray, talk, and look at God's handiwork starts our day in the right direction. If for any reason, we have to miss this "morning start-up" it seems that the travel through the day is filled with too many bumps and detours.

When we had been married 36 years, we were to do a workshop on "marriage" so we prepared a list of "36 things we have learned in 36 years of marriage." Each year we added something else to the list. Although we are in our 47th year, we have only 46 items, as we do not add the extra lesson until the year is over. Here is the list for you:

46 THINGS WE HAVE LEARNED IN 46 YEARS OF MARRIAGE
Charles and Louise Cox

1. The fact that marriage doesn't turn out to be what you thought it was like during courtship doesn't mean it's not great.
2. Romance is as important after 46 years of marriage as it was at the beginning. If it's become a way of life with the two of you, it's not difficult.
3. Neither of us is ALWAYS right or ALWAYS wrong, but each of us is sometimes right and sometimes wrong.
4. TIME is one of the most precious things in marriage and often it is the most difficult to come by. When we work together on a chore of any kind, it makes the time go by more quickly and gives us another opportunity for time together.
5. Just because one of us tells the other something, that doesn't necessarily mean the other one hears what we've said.
6. Making a home and a marriage is a dual responsibility.
7. When one of us fails in the responsibility that is ours, we have weakened the marriage structure.
8. If you want to stay at "odds" with one another. try playing the "I'll get even game."

9. Your lifestyle won't always please your family and friends, but then you are not married to them.

10. Taking God in as a partner in marriage makes the marriage better in every way.

11. Love is more than a word you say or a feeling you have; it is the attitude and action in your daily lives.

12. Many marriages "give out" because neither partner will "give in."

13. Money doesn't buy happiness, but it helps keep a roof over your head. Money is not the evil; the love of it is, and the love of it reaches rich and poor alike.

14. Perfection has not existed on this earth since the days of Jesus Christ; it will not begin with either of us.

15. When you use one another's strengths, you minimize your own weaknesses and those of your partner.

16. A soft answer will turn away wrath, but no answer at all can be very irritating.

17. Togetherness is very important, but we each need "breathing room." The individualism given us by God is also important.

18. By changing ourselves we often change our mates.

19. A kind, loving word or a thoughtful act is more precious than an expensive gift or a dozen roses.

20. The nutrition of well-balanced meals is important, but so is the well-balanced life — one balanced with work, play and worship, as well as relaxation.

21. Start your day by reading the Bible and praying together, and you are better prepared to handle whatever the day may bring.

22. A man and a woman do not think the same way about many things. It is when neither of them think of the other that trouble starts.

23. When something "bugs" you, it is best to get it out in the open (in a kindly manner) and exterminate it before it eats away at your marriage like termites in a house.

24. Marriage calls for each one to learn how to love "in spite of" and not only "because of."

25. Sometimes a deep and meaningful silence says more than an hour or more of conversation.

26. "Housekeepers" can be hired; "homemakers" cannot.

27. When each one of you wants the OTHER'S happiness more than you want YOUR OWN, you are BOTH happier.

28. The problems you face and the storms you have to weather make your marriage stronger. A marriage without problems would be like a year without rain — too much sun would destroy the growth. It helps us to realize we need God on both good days and bad.

29. A sense of humor will be one of the most essential tools you have in your "homemaking kit." Using it often does many things: it opens tightly closed doors, hardened hearts, and soothes aches and pains. It is often used to wipe away tears. "A merry heart doeth good like a medicine."

30. Marriage is like a play; we each have definite roles to play. If either of us gets "out of character" or "forgets our lines"; then we've thrown the whole act out of balance.

31. Marriage is like a football team. It is a winning team when there is good teamwork and good sportsmanship and when the ball is not fumbled. These are more important than keeping score.

32. "I love you" is something to be said often, but it should be put in practice constantly and consistently.

33. The husband is to be the "head of the home;" the wife is to be the "heart of the home." They are equally important roles. A heart without a head would be out of control. A head without a heart would be lifeless and inadequate. Together they make a more perfect union.

34. All the "things" we accumulate require effort to keep them in shape to be used. Too many "things" leave no time or space for the more important aspects of marriage.

35. The closer you both become to God, the closer you grow to one another.

36. Marriage is like a balancing act; it must be balanced with not too many friends, nor too few; not too much involvement with work, nor too little; not too much concern for one's self, but not too little either; not too much recreation, but not too little.

37. It takes a lot of four letter words to make a marriage what it should be — words like "love, care, work, time, pray, hope, help."

38. Marriage upsets all you've ever learned about Math. In marriage two people become one. By dividing sorrows, troubles, chores and difficulties you find you are multiplying joys and happiness. This division also subtracts loneliness and uncertainty and adds to one's trust in God and one another.

39. Have you ever noticed how much further OUR money goes than YOUR money or MY MONEY?

40. You make history as you live together as man and wife. You don't write that history by repeating the same mistakes over and over, or by continually bringing up the past mistakes of your mate. Instead you edit each page carefully, taking out the unnecessary and adding the important.

41. WHERE you live is much less important than HOW you live.

42. The husband who sees his role as only that of being "a breadwinner and bringing home the bacon" is like someone blind in one eye, the wife who sees her husband in only the role of breadwinner and bacon bringer is like someone totally blind.

43. Even burned toast can be delicious if love shares the table.

44. You both must learn to love people and use things instead of the other way around.

45. Turn your marriage over to God, and He will direct your steps.

46. A good and happy marriage doesn't come cheap. It costs us the best we have to give. Yet, compared with an unhappy marriage and/or a divorce, it is one of the greatest bargains to be found anywhere.

After 46 years our middles are thicker, our hair is thinner, our steps are slower, our eyes are dimmer, our hearing less acute, but our love is stronger, our judgment wiser, our patience greater, and our marriage better than ever.

It's been a good 46 years, but not without problems, mistakes, sorrows, hardships and heartaches. But they fade in light of the joys, rewards, and peace of mind that comes from the strength we have through Christ through whom we can do all things, even make a good marriage better.

FOR THOUGHT AND DISCUSSION

1. Share something that you practice that has made your marriage stronger.

2. What do you consider the greatest problem in today's marriages? What can be done to resolve the problem?

3. Discuss "the church as the bride of Christ" and make a comparison between the things that strengthen and weaken that relationship that can be paralleled in our marriages.

4. Choose five wives we read about in the Bible and discuss their strengths and their weaknesses as wives.

FOR YOUR PERSONAL USE

1. Make a written list of the things you appreciate in your husband.

2. Give him a bouquet from the garden of your heart by telling him (either personally or in a note) what you appreciate.

3. List five of your own faults which create difficulties in your marriage. Choose one and work on ridding yourself of it.

4. Tell your husband you love him.

5. Make a date with your husband (get a sitter). Go out for a ride, a hamburger, or a candlelight dinner, and talk about the especially happy times you have shared.

6. If your husband is under stress because of health, business pressure, or finances, find some small thing you can do to relieve that stress and DO IT.

MY PRAYER FOR YOU

Dear God, we thank you for your wisdom in creating us with a purpose for our lives. Help us to fulfill that purpose with love for you and our husbands. Give us courage, wisdom, strength to become the kind of wives who will help husbands to become all you want them to be. May we seek for understanding, joy, peace, love, communication, spiritual strength, commitment, and happiness for our husbands, knowing that when it comes to them, it comes to us also. In Jesus name.

Amen

CHAPTER 9

BLOOM WHERE YOU ARE PLANTED AS A MOTHER

Introduction:

Can you think of a more important work that can be done than to be the right kind of parent for a God-given child?

Perhaps I feel this more keenly than many because I have no children of my own. A miscarriage early in my marriage left me unable to bear children. A later attempt at adoption was thwarted when the child we were to have adopted was kidnapped by its father and taken to Mexico. Since then we have given ourselves to working with children and young people. It cuts my heart to the core to hear of child neglect, child abuse, and unconcerned parents.

The purpose of this chapter is to look at the charge given to mothers (and fathers) through the scriptures, to look at some Biblical mothers and their examples, and to record some information gained from those who are now mothers. Such a review we hope will enable each of us to develop a broader view of the role of the mother and her importance to her child or children. We would also hope that it will offer encouragement and help to develop a deep sense of gratitude in the hearts of those who are privileged to be mothers, so that they might more easily bloom where they are planted.

The Biblical Perspective of Parenthood (Especially Motherhood)

In keeping with the theme of a "rose garden," we need to prepare properly the soil for effective parenthood. A single verse of scripture, if properly applied, might prevent many problems with rearing children. It is:

"He that loveth father or mother more than me is not worthy of me; and he that loveth son or daughter more than me is not worthy of me." (Matthew 10:37)

If our allegiance and love come to God and Christ FIRST, then our relationships with our families are going to be what God intends them to be. Unfortunately, it is much easier for all of us to seek to please our children (or our parents) rather than to please God. Discuss.

Proverbs 22:6

> *"Train up a child in the way he should go; and when he is old, he will not depart from it."*

This is a familiar verse, but do we understand what it DOES NOT say as clearly as we understand what it DOES say? Note: It does not specify that only a father or only a mother should train up a child. It takes both parents to give the child the well-rounded training necessary to function as a Christian while living in the world. It takes both parents training the child to help fortify him or her against peer pressure. So neither parent has the right to shift all the responsibility to the other.

Note further: The verse DOES NOT say a child will **never** depart from his training. It says, "when he is old, he will not depart from it." As we grow older, we grow wiser; but as children and youths we often lack the wisdom and the maturity to travel the right paths. That is why it is so urgent that parents "be there" and be constant and consistent in their training of the child.

We often see young people who have been brought up in so-called Christian homes who are not yet able to discern good from evil. This could be the result of three failures on the part of a mother (or a father):

(1)   Failure to train a child in the way in which he should go.
(2)   Teaching a child facts without helping that child to learn to apply those facts to his or her life.
(3)   Failing to set a proper example — talking one way and walking another.

But just as important as these three failures is the danger of the parent who considers making all a child's decisions as the proper way to train. This leaves the child to grow into youth and adulthood without ever providing opportunity for that child to "exercise his or her senses to discern both good and evil." It is keeping the child on a milk diet long after that child is ready for strong meat. Few would cause their child's death by denying the child proper physical food, but what about lack of spiritual food?

There is probably no one who will read this book who believes more firmly than I do, the need for good influence in the life of a child and young person as provided by the church and our Christian institutions of learning. Yet neither can be a substitute for the on-hands training done by parents. The church and Christian institutions of learning are reinforcements to God's command to "train up a child in the way he should go." They are built upon foundations laid by parents. But a child turned loose when he is two cannot be expected to be turned into the model child at age 18. The age of miracles has passed.

Proverbs 22:15

> *"Foolishness is bound in the heart of a child; but the rod of correction shall drive it far from him."*

How clearly this indicates that a child's judgment is not mature and that correction is essential if the child is to mature properly. "The rod of correction" does not mean child abuse; it means loving a child enough to have the courage to punish when punishment is needed.

Ecclesiastes 4:13

> *"Better is a poor and a wise child than an old and foolish king, who will no more be admonished."*

A parent I know who has experienced many problems with her daughter said in tears, "We always gave her everything that money could buy, but we never gave her the training and discipline she needed. Now we are paying a high price for our mistake."

How is a child to know what God expects of him or her unless that child is taught. Let's look at some instructions to children and ask ourselves, honestly, what we as parents and other adults are doing to help children and young people to know, believe, and practice these admonitions from the scriptures:

1. *Exodus 20:12:* "Honor thy father and mother . . . ."
2. *Psalm 148:12, 13:* "Both young men, and maidens, old men and children: Let them praise the name of the Lord; for his name alone is excellent; his glory is above the earth and heaven."
3. *Proverbs 1:8:* "My son, hear the instruction of thy father, and forsake not the law of thy mother."

4. *Proverbs 23:22:* "Harken unto thy father that begat thee, and despise not thy mother when she is old."
5. *Ephesians 6:1:* "Children, obey your parents in the Lord, for this is right . . . ."

Five short verses, yet within them lie the difference in being pleasing to God or displeasing. Children cannot know and understand unless we, as parents and adults, are willing to make the effort to teach them.

I heard a teacher in a teen-age girls' class make a wise statement: "You may not understand this until you are older, but there will come a time when you will remember it. When you live as God wants you to, whatever your age, your life will be far less complicated than if you try to do your own thing."

Look at a newborn child — small, helpless, defenseless, teachable. What a wonderful gift from God to parents who can devote themselves to seeing that their child grows as Jesus grew, "mentally, physically, spiritually and socially." When one phase of the four-part growth is neglected, the other three are penalized.

A Biblical Example of a Mother Who Bloomed Where She Was Planted

Read carefully II Kings 4:8-37. This is one of my favorite Biblical accounts of a woman's life. In such a few verses we are confronted with all our human excuses and a woman who wipes them away as if they did not exist. She is too busy blooming where she is planted to be caught in the dangerous web of "I can't, because . . . ."

Let's look at some vital points:

(1) Verse 8 - We learn in this verse that this was a woman of Shunam. We learn that she was a great woman. We do not know her name, and commentators differ as to whether great referred to her wealth or her character. The lesson for mothers is that one may be a great mother without being wealthy or getting publicity for it. In the verse we also learn that she was hospitable. She invited Elisha in to eat bread. It does not say she worked for days preparing an elaborate feast. She saw an opportunity to be hospitable and grasped it. How much children need to see the quality of hospitality in their parents.

(2) Verses 9-10: The Shunammite woman saw a need and had an idea. How much we, as women, need these qualities — a sensitivity to the needs of others and creativity to develop ideas to meet needs. She discussed the idea with her husband. There is the importance of good communication. Then she prepared a simple place for Elisha to rest overnight with bed, table, stool and candlestick, giving no excuse for what she didn't have, but making available graciously what she did have.

(3) Verses 12-17: What a beautiful example of contentment in the life of a woman is found in these verses. Here Elisha wants to express his gratitude for her hospitality. He offers to speak to the king or the captain in her behalf. The Shunammite woman answers simply, " I dwell among mine own people." Contrast that with modern-day excuses, "I would do more, but nobody appreciates it." Or "I have done so much for so many and no one does anything for me." What greater characteristic can a woman possess than to be content. It enhances her own life, but it also enhances the lives of members of her family and friends.

It was Elisha's servant Gehazi who suggested that this woman had no child and that might be a gift she would appreciate. Elisha called her to him and told her that she would soon bear a child. She doubted this because her husband was quite old.

But she did conceive and bore the child. Please note that she did not change her lifestyle. How often we hear women say, "I can't do this or that because I have a child." "I can't put my husband first because my child has so many needs."

The child grew, and one day he went into the field with his father and the reapers. Perhaps the Shunammite women made this time for father and son to be together. How much better it is for a mother to make such time than to complain that the father spends no time with the children.

But the boy became ill, and the father had a servant take him back to his mother. Modern woman might well have commented, "I knew I shouldn't let him go," or "Your father is so irresponsible that he can't look after you for even a few minutes. If I had been there, this wouldn't have happened." It is said "little pitchers have big ears." Think about this. If a child hears a mother speak of the father in this manner, how is that child going to know how to "honor thy father?" The Shunammite woman was different!

Once again she followed the same pattern: She saw a need, she planned how it could be handled, she discussed it with the father, and she took action. (Verses 20-24). Note also another thing that shows her ability to bloom where she was planted as a mother. She did not ask for special consideration from the servant. She kept her eyes on the goal. Her concern was for others.

The Shunammite woman had her priorities in order: God first, then husband, child, others, self. To each of these, in a very direct and simple way, she offered a bouquet from her heart's garden of love; she bloomed where she was planted and through the years the fragrance of her bloom has affected the lives of many other mothers and wives.

We do not know her name, she cared not for fame and recognition, yet she lives in our hearts.

Some Mothers I Have Known

As a springboard to this section of this chapter, try this exercise. Think of someone you consider to be an outstanding mother. Write down three qualities that are visible in her life that help to make her outstanding.

1. _____

2. _____

3. _____

Now ask yourself what others would consider your outstanding characteristics as mother.

You notice that I use many modern-day examples in this book. I do this because, as I have taught through the years, I have often been confronted with the comment, "Yeah, but the women we read about in the Bible were different. We can't be like they were." My examples are intended to help you realize that it is possible to "bloom where you are planted as a mother anywhere in the world and at any time in which you may live." But there is no way you can do it alone; you need God's help.

Meet Three of My Favorite Mothers

First, I will introduce my own mother, now deceased. No one has ever had the influence on me that she had and continues to have. Hers was not an easy life, but she never failed to bloom where she was planted. She touched, not only my life, but the lives of many of my friends and certainly the life of my husband, who loved her dearly.

Perhaps the best way for me to share the fragrance of her Heart's Bouquet with you is to share with you two things I wrote about her before she died.

Mother believed that we must learn to make very practical application of the scriptures to our daily lives. She had the knack of getting a point across to her children that they would long remember. I wrote the following article which appeared in the TRIBUNE NEWS, Cartersville, Ga. on December 19,1980.

THREE THINGS MY MOTHER TAUGHT ME

Do you ever stop to think how many things you were taught as a youngster that have stood the test of time?

There are three things my mother taught me (often repeating them until I wished she'd forget them) that I find useful on almost a daily basis:

1. "If you stay busy enough with the DO'S of this life, you won't have to worry about the DON'TS."
2. "The best way to show that a stick is crooked is to lay a straight one down beside it."
3. "Your abilities plus your opportunities equal your responsibilities."

A lot of water has gone over the dam and many things have changed, but these three points remain as true as when I first learned them.

And so does a bit of advice she used to give me when I was inclined to 'jump to conclusions.'

'Opinions first; facts last; and so confusion.' Perhaps one day we will reverse the order and get understanding."

SHE IS AND SHE ISN'T

(Lines written to my mother, Vida Pittman Barnett on her 88th Birthday).

My mother is no longer young, as we know youth today,
But the years have touched her gently as they've passed her on the way.

My mother has no claim to fame for one award or another.
She gave up what she "might have been" to be a wife and mother.

My mother has no selfish strain to make her seek her own;
Instead she's always given of herself to all whom she has known.

My mother has no brave philosophy, just a trusting faith in God.
She never brought us up by "Dr. Spock;" she simply used "the rod."

My mother cannot paint or write or sing, but she can stew and broil and bake.
And what is even more, my friend, she can soothe one's hurt and ache.

My mother's world is not so very wide, but she counts friends by the score,
And they know they'll find a welcome when they knock upon her door.

My mother will never be a genius, but she has a heart of gold,
She's ever busy cheering others with deeds of kindness oft untold.

My mother is no great intellectual, but she has the gift of chatter.
In fact, she can go on and on 'til you wonder what's the matter.

My mother cannot get about too well and spends much time alone,
But when she counts her blessings, I hope she counts the phone.

My mother isn't many, many things, but the lady's quite a whiz!
I can't be counting what she ISN'T — I'm too glad of WHAT SHE IS!

A Mother Planted in a Different Garden

The second modern-day mother is my friend Rosemary Whittle McKnight. She is a writer who almost literally pushed me into writing this book. She is a teacher and her husband is currently working on his doctorate. They live with her parents with their two sons. Rosemary could have handled this lifestyle differently, but she weaves her role as a mother into all else she does, and her children are richer for it.

As I worked on this chapter, I asked her to tell me three things that she felt were important for mothers to do, if they were to "bloom where they are planted." Here are three things she is doing.

94

Rosemary said, "I wanted to improve my own prayer life, and, as I began my work on that, I realized I needed to help my children improve theirs. Each night when I hear them say their prayers, we talk about a prayer list and the things that we have for which to be thankful. My son, Jonathan, is seven. Imagine how I felt when one night recently he prayed, "Thank you God for all the people who have lived to be over 100. They haven't smoked, used alcohol, or drugs, and they have stayed strong." Never in my entire life had I thought to pray such a prayer."

She continued, "Perhaps it is living with my parents that makes me realize how much older people enjoy young children. So when I make visits to shut-ins, the ill, or to nursing homes, I take my children. After a series of such visits, Jonathan said, "Mother, I'm glad I got to meet those ladies. It is nice to know some of the people I have been praying for.""

Then Rosemary said she believed it was vitally important for parents to know their children's friends. She said, "You cannot do this unless you are willing to get involved with their friends. Gary and I are currently doing this in a number of ways. I am a room mother, Gary and I work with the Cub Scouts, and Gary and my dad coach a Little League team. This way we become involved with our children and their friends. I like to think we influence both our children and their friends."

Rosemary is a mother who doesn't have to have the perfect setting to bloom where she is planted; she blooms wherever she finds herself. She shares her Heart's Bouquet with her family, the church, and the community.

The Difficult Role of a Single Mother

Another very special friend of mine is a single parent — Linda Helm. She is not filling this role as a single parent by choice, but by circumstances beyond her control. She has a young son, Jonathan.

She teaches full time, is active in the work of the church and is continuing her education. How does she find time to bloom?

She is well-organized and understands what it means to "redeem the time." I have never known her to miss an opportunity to be thoughtful, never in big, showy ways, but always in small, meaningful ways. She is teaching her son, Jonathan, to do the same thing.

She reaches out to people instead of waiting for them to seek her out. She helps Jonathan to be friends of her friends, as she is friends with his friends. Caring is an important part of her Heart's Bouquet that she shares continually.

She never presents her former husband in a bad light to her son. She says, "Divorce is difficult enough for a child to understand and handle without my adding bitterness or a feeling that he has to 'choose' between us." Linda might well be called a "good-finder" — she looks for the good in everyone. She says, "No matter what our circumstances, I want Jonathan to know God's World is wonderful and the Christian life is great."

She is trying to give her son security, training, and the feeling of balance in his life.

Advice From an Expert

Since I have no children of my own, I dare to give advice freely. I will not have to eat my words.

Here are some pieces of advice I would offer from my vantage point, that of a non-mother with a close relationship with many children and young people of all ages.

1. Teach your child about God as soon as he or she comes into the world.

2. Let your child see you living the life you are asking it to live; your child knows that a double standard is no bargain.

3. Lead your child to Christ; don't drive him away. God gave each of us the freedom to choose whether or not we follow Christ. You cannot make that choice for your child; you can only guide and pray.

4. The child who runs wild at age 2 in open rebellion will not change at 22, unless you provide a proper direction at an early age.

5. Use the Bible as your road map for your child's travel through life and for your own journey. Help your child make wise decisions; don't make them for him. Guide him into making good decisions.

6. Hold your child accountable. God does.

7. Remember that love, discipline, and spiritual guidance will mean more to your child than any heritage you can leave.

8. Don't confuse "quantity" with "quality" in the time you spend with your child.

9. Count your blessings that God has entrusted a tiny life into your hands to bring up to full adulthood to be all that God would have that life to be.

10. Learn to share your heart's bouquet with your child in simple ways and help that child learn to do the same.

FOR THOUGHT AND DISCUSSION

1. Discuss the wisdom that can be seen in God's instructions to parents, and discuss how God's way can be proven the best way.

2. Openly discuss the problems children and young people face in today's world, and make suggestions as to how not only parents, but all adults, may be of help to the children and youth.

3. Name at least five things to which your child is exposed which are often in direct conflict with God's way. How can these influences best be handled?

1._____

2._____

3._____

4._____

5._____

FOR YOUR PRIVATE AND PERSONAL USE

1. Study carefully the role God has planned for you as a mother. Make notes and plans for becoming the mother God wants you to be.

2. Try very hard to present the Christian life to your child (by both what you say and what you do) as a beautiful life that far surpasses any other choice of lifestyle.

3. Improve your communication skills. Learn to listen well so that you will know your child's spoken and unspoken needs. Give praise, instructions, criticism, and discipline in sincere love and concern for the welfare of your child. Improve your communication with God through an improved prayer life. We all need God — but especially parents.

MY PRAYER FOR YOU

Dear Father, help me to be the kind of child that you would have me be, so that I may better teach my child what he or she should be. Help me to pray as did Your Son "Nevertheless, not my will, but Thine be done" as I struggle with the awe-inspiring task of rearing my children.

Help me, Father, to give to my child, as you have given to me, patience, understanding, guidance, mercy, and forgiveness. In Jesus Name.

In Jesus' name, Amen

CHAPTER 10

BLOOM WHERE YOU ARE PLANTED
AS A MOTHER OF TEENAGERS

Introduction:

It has been my experience that teenagers can tell whether the roses in our heart's bouquets are real or artificial more quickly than any other group. This is why I have chosen to add this particular chapter.

The purpose of this chapter is to help each of us, whether we are mothers or those who work with teens, to recognize the masks they wear, the world in which they live, the pressures they face daily, the deep (often unspoken) needs they have, and how often they relate to the Apostle Paul's dilemma of "what I would, that I do not; but what I hate, I do."

A friend of mine, Fran Elrod, of Cartersville, Georgia, has taught teen-age girls for a number of years. Once she expressed what most of us have felt at times when she said, "I look at them and what I see is that they are in an ocean too deep for them, and they are crying for help. I am standing on shore trying desperately to throw a rope with a life preserver to them. But my rope is not long enough." What she means is that we are going to have to study God's Word more, develop our spiritual qualities to a higher level and have the courage to do whatever is needed to help those who are in water over their heads. Personally, I agree with her. We will never be able to help our teenagers by standing on the shore. I believe we are going to have the courage to launch out into the deep where the storms really are. We must launch out with the positive faith that "Peter's Lord is our Lord, too," and sometimes only He can calm the storm.

To quote my friend, Ben Flatt, minister for Henderson Church of Christ, Henderson, TN, "We must realize that when God says DO something, we must DO IT. When God says DON'T DO something, we must NOT DO IT." How much we need to get this message over to teens, not only by our teaching, but also by our daily example.

May this chapter help us learn to 'bloom where we are planted" by preparing a peaceful garden haven to which we may bring them after we launch out and save them. But may it also help us to prepare so that we ourselves will not drown in our efforts to save our teenagers. Without the help of God it cannot happen. But the same Lord who calmed the storm for Peter will help us calm the storms for our teenagers and for ourselves, if we will only let Him.

Back to Basics

In our efforts to give the young people of today more and greater opportunities than we had growing up, we have, in many instances, robbed them of their childhood and youth. At 6 they are trying to cope with adult problems, and in their teens they are old — not in years, but in terms of knowledge of the wrong things, worries, fears, indecisions and broken lives.

You and I may stand on the shore hoping to rescue them and help them find a haven filled with flowers in our heart's gardens. Our young people may want that haven desperately. But until both we and they have the courage to make the right moves, neither of us will be able to reach the other.

And where do we learn the right moves? We must go back to the basics, the basics that are found in God's Word. The following verses, chosen at random, can help provide a firm foundation on which to build as we seek to get back to basics.

As you read each of these verses, discuss them in class. But, do even more; discuss them with teenagers as you try to help them strengthen their faith and give them something unchangeable to hold onto in an ever-changing world.

> *Nahum 1:7.* "The Lord is good, a strong hold in the day of trouble; and he knoweth them that trust in him."
>
> *Matthew 11:28.* "Come unto me, all ye that labor and are heavy-laden and I will give you rest."
>
> *John 14:1.* "Let not your heart be troubled; ye believe in God, believe also in me."
>
> *Romans 8:28.* "... We know that all things work together for good to them that love God, to them who are the called according to his purpose."

II Corinthians 4:8. "We are troubled on every side, yet not distressed; we are perplexed, but not in despair."

Hebrews 13:6. ". . . the Lord is my helper and I will not fear what any man shall do unto me."

James 1:12. "Blessed is the man that endureth temptation; for when he is tried, he shall receive the crown of life, which the Lord hath promised to them that love him."

Matthew 16:26. "What is a man profited if he shall gain the whole world and lose his own soul? or what shall a man give in exchange for his soul?"

I John 2:16. ". . . all that is in the world, the lust of the flesh, and the lust of the eyes, and the pride of life, is not of the Father, but is of the world."

Proverbs 30:33. "Surely the churning of milk bringeth forth butter, and the wringing of the nose bringeth forth blood; so the forcing of wrath bringeth forth strife."

Ephesians 4:14-15. "That we henceforth be no more children, tossed to and fro, and carried about with every wind of doctrine, by the sleight of men, and cunning craftiness, whereby they lie in wait to deceive: But speaking the truth in love, may grow up into him in all things, which is the head, even Christ."

Ephesians 4:32. ". . . be ye kind one to another, tenderhearted, forgiving one another, even as God for Christ's sake hath forgiven you."

Proverbs 3:5. "Trust in the Lord with all thine heart; and lean not unto thy own understanding."

Proverbs 3:7. "Be not wise in thine own eyes; fear the Lord and depart form evil."

I Timothy 6:6. ". . . godliness with contentment is great gain."

Luke 6:31. ". . . as ye would that men should do to you, do ye also to them likewise."

Romans 13:9. ". . . Thou shalt not commit adultery, thou shalt not kill, thou shalt not steal, thou shalt not bear false witness, thou shalt not covet; and if there be any other commandment, it is briefly comprehended in this saying, namely, Thou shalt love thy neighbor as thyself."

I Corinthians 10:13. "There hath no temptation taken you but such as is common to man: but God is faithful, who will not suffer you to be tempted above that ye are able; but will with the temptation also make a way to escape, that ye may be able to bear it."

II Timothy 2:22. "Flee also youthful lusts: but follow righteousness, faith, charity, peace, with them that call on the Lord out of a pure heart."

I Timothy 4:12. "Let no man despise thy youth; but be thou an example of the believers, in word, in conversation, in charity, in spirit, in faith, purity."

II Timothy 1:7. "For God hath not given us the spirit of fear; but of power, and of love, and of a sound mind."

These are only a few of the scriptures that might have been chosen, but they will provide much food for thought. As you discuss each individual scripture, discuss it from the standpoint of how it can help you as a mother of teenagers to cope and also how it can help your teenager to cope.

Temptation Has Been Around A Long Time

We tend to assume that temptations are greater today than ever before. Statistics would probably prove that there are more temptations for teens and that the world has become more adept at packaging them attractively than ever before. But the Bible contains many accounts of temptations that are similar to some we see today. Let's look at a few.

Have someone tell briefly the account of Cain and Abel. This brings some familiar temptations — sibling rivalry. It went uncontrolled and led to murder. Another similarity that can be seen is that Abel listened to God, but Cain did not. Cain opted to "do his own thing." Each time I read the account and think about it, I cannot help but recall that Eve did not provide a good foundation for coping with such problems. In her sin we see evidences of jealousy, or envy, wanting more than her portion and of "doing her own thing."

Have someone briefly recall the account of Rebekah's helping Jacob to deceive Isaac. Think about that in the terms of today. Do mothers ever help their children deceive their fathers, perhaps by helping them to slip around to do something that the fathers have forbidden? But what of Esau? He did not know how to value his birthright and so was willing to sell it. How many teens do you know who have been willing to sell their claim to a pure life in order to enjoy "the pleasures of sin for a season."

Have someone tell the story of Joseph and Potiphar's wife. Notice that temptation could be resisted then and it can be resisted now. It takes faith in God and courage and determination.

Sin Wears Dress Clothes, Not Overalls

Looking at the problem of being the mother of a teen-ager and blooming where you are planted calls for two things to begin with:

(1) The spiritual quality of your own life must provide a good role model.

(2) You must learn (and help your teen to learn) that SIN rarely appears wearing dirty clothes, workclothes, or overalls. It more often appears in handsome clothes, brightly colored and up-to-the-minute in fashion. It is attractively packaged and usually focuses on whatever is "IN" at the moment. It is an artificial bouquet, but it can appear very real.

Think of the amount of time available for you to spend with your teen-agers. Compare that with the number of hours in which they may be influenced by peers, society as a whole, TV, reading materials, and so-called "heroes" from the world of entertainment, sports, and other activities. This is why it is so urgent that you bloom where you are planted each moment of your day. You must offer your teen-agers guidance toward building a stronger faith, learning how to avoid giving in to temptations, assuming responsibilities, doing unto others as they would have others do unto them, and going God's way instead of their own. In doing so you are sharing your heart's bouquet that will spill a fragrance in every corner of their lives. Think how important it is for you to teach them the same things we've talked about earlier about preparing the soil, planting, weeding, and sharing their hearts' bouquets.

From the Inside Instead of the Outside

Teen-agers are skilled at hurting on the inside and wearing a smile on the outside. They often express needs that are nothing more than cover-ups for real needs. Rebellious behavior may be a silent cry for love, help, and acceptance.

Rarely a week passes that I do not receive a letter, or a phone call or have someone talk with me about problems. Most often these are young people and their parents. They want a listening ear and they want someone they can trust. As I have worked on this chapter, I've tried to list the most frequent problems that are called to my attention:

FROM YOUNG PEOPLE:

Lack of self-esteem, insecurity
Sex
Money
Drugs
Drinking
Their relationships with God, their families, their friends
Peer pressure
Wanting to be a better person, but not knowing how
Divorce in their family
Loss of a friend
Breakup with a boyfriend or girlfriend
Fear of war, earthquake, and other disasters
Dating
Problems in school
Feeling that parents don't care

FROM PARENTS:

Feeling that God has forsaken them because of the problems they face
Personal conflicts in the home
Inability to understand young people
Peer pressure
Materialism
Fear of disciplining their children
The heartache and sense of failure that comes when a child "goes bad"

Since I have no background in counseling, I feel I have but a few choices on how to handle these confidences. Perhaps they will help you:

1. Listen attentively.

2. Keep confidences.

3. Offer encouragement where possible.

4. Read the Bible and pray with them.

5. Express your love for the person, but your extreme unhappiness for the sin in their lives.

6. Suggest professional counseling, if needed.

7. Keep communication lines open and offer sincere friendship.

8. Refuse to let them use you as a crutch.

9. Pray for them privately and encourage them at every opportunity.

10. Be the best role model you know how to be.

My husband and I, for years, have been very upset by the mass condemnation of young people we hear so often. Sure, there are a few really bad young people, and they are usually the most visible, vocal and obvious. They go in for the shock treatment and gain notoriety because of it.

Yet for the small number who follow this path, there is a larger number who yearn for guidance, love, and something on which to pin their hope for the future. Their problem is they don't know where and how to find it. There is an even larger group who are "good young people." They may not make the headlines, but they are helping to make the world a better place. We need to reach out and give each of these groups a bouquet of love from our hearts, patterned after the love God has shown to us. And if we need to leave the safety of the shore and swim into the deep and turbulent water to guide them to a safe haven, where they can enjoy our hearts' gardens, then we must be willing to bloom where we are planted by preparing that haven.

Read the Bible and you will find that "encouragement" and "edification" are key words throughout. That is something we need, no matter what our age. But it is a deep need for teens. It works with the rebellious, those who are struggling to find their way, and those who have begun living faithful to Jesus at an early age. But if it is to be effective, the rose of encouragement from your heart must be real and sincere and not artificial.

It has been said, "A pat on the back will take a fellow much farther than a kick in the pants." As the mother of a teen-ager, wouldn't you agree that it takes some of both, but more pats than kicks?

Take it to the Lord in Prayer

I asked several mothers of teens what they felt they needed most to handle the challenges of being a mother to a teen-age child. Here are the things that surfaced most often in the conversations:

1. God's help

2. Wisdom

3. Patience

4. A strong prayer life

If it is God's help we seek, He stands willing and able to give it. We obtain it from a study of God's Word, an application of that Word to every phase of our lives. It must also help us to develop that TOTAL trust in God that is necessary if we are to "bloom where we are planted," no matter how difficult the circumstances.

If it is wisdom we seek, then we need to read and believe and practice James 1:5-8: "If any of you lack wisdom, let him ask of God that giveth to all men liberally, and upbraideth not; and it shall be given him. But let him ask in faith, nothing wavering. For he that wavereth is like a wave of the sea driven with the wind and tossed. For let not that man think he shall receive anything of the Lord. A double-minded man is unstable in his ways."

If it is patience we seek, let us think of the patience God has with us. How often we are like teenagers, trying God's patience daily. Our trials help us to develop patience. As one mother said, "I asked God for patience and He gave me three teenagers."

If it is a strong prayer life you seek, take it to the Lord in prayer. Pray with and for your teen-ager. Talk to God as you would talk with a close friend. He will not betray your confidence and He will help you in ways nobody else can.

FOR THOUGHT AND DISCUSSION

1. Find a verse of scripture that has proven helpful to you in establishing better relationships with teens. Read in class.

2. How can parents and the church work together to help the teenagers see this period of their lives as a meaningful and happy time, instead of a troubled and terrible time?

FOR YOUR PERSONAL USE

Once I heard of a family who set aside one night per week as "family night." The mother planned favorite dishes and set the table as if for important guests. The father and the children helped with the meal and did the "clean-up." No TV was permitted. At each plate there was an envelope with a "rose sticker and the person's name" on it. Inside each member of the family had put in a sentence that said "A rose to you this week because of..." Then they listed something that was good that the person to whom the note was addressed had done and signed their name. Each person read his notes aloud to the group. The evening was spent in conversation, playing games together and being a family. It was closed with a devotional which included scripture readings, perhaps an application story, songs, and prayer.

Another thing you might wish to do is to scan the first five chapters of this book again and see if you need to help your teen-ager(s) Tear Down Those Fences, Prepare the Soil, Plants Seeds of Knowledge to Reap a Harvest of Wisdom, Refuse to Plant Poison Ivy in Their Rose Gardens, and to Weed and Prune. Help them to learn to "bloom where they are planted" as teen-agers.

MY PRAYER FOR YOU

Dear Heavenly Father, please be with parents of teenagers the world over. Give them wisdom, patience, courage and, love to rear these young people as You would have them do.

Help them to impart a love for You and others to these teens that they, too, may love God and fellowman.

May every parent learn to give "good gifts" to their children, as You so bountifully give good gifts to us. May some of these gifts be a strong sense of values, a feeling of worth as Your creation, discipline and praise, a willingness to work and to assume responsibility. May parents also give their children time and attention, a listening ear, a desire for Truth, and a realization that "With Christ there is an endless hope, but without him, there is a hopeless end."

Help those of us who work with teens to provide love, encouragement, and support to both the teens and their parents as we all work together to make the world a better place. In Jesus' name.

Amen

CHAPTER 11

BLOOM WHERE YOU ARE PLANTED
EVEN IN THE EMPTY NEST

Introduction:

The idea for this chapter in HEART'S BOUQUET came as I was having lunch with a friend in a nice tearoom. At the table next to us were two well-dressed women. One of them was talking in such clear tones she could be heard distinctly at our table. In essence, here is what she was saying, "I feel as free as a bird. My last child has married and moved out and I am delighted. Just think - I won't have to consider anyone except myself. I won't have to be involved in church work to set a good example. I won't have to be involved in school and community. I won't have to plan my schedule to match theirs, I won't have to put up with their friends. I can do as I please, when I please. I plan to spend my time shopping, partying, playing golf with my husband and we will travel extensively. I am so excited."

As she spoke, I thought of the three different ways in which mothers approach "the empty nest" when their children have all left home.

(1) They can, as this mother, succumb to the disease of 'selfishness' which is painful and deadly;

(2) They can succumb to an equally deadly disease that also progresses rapidly, "apathy"; or

(3) They can recognize that the "empty nest" is a normal phase of life and remain healthy, happy, and unselfish as they embark on a different course from any they have known before.

When one is left with the empty nest, it is much like the vacant spaces that occur in our rose gardens when we lose certain plants or they quit blooming for a season. How tragic when the diseases of selfishness and apathy attack a mother in this stage of life and result in even more vacant spots in her rose garden.

The purpose of this chapter is to help mothers cope with the empty nest syndrome. In order to do this, we will need to look at several things: symptoms of the diseases of both selfishness and apathy, how to control the diseases, and how to fill the empty spots in our gardens that we may live abundantly even in an empty nest.

Vacant Spots in Our Gardens

Avid gardeners know that, despite all efforts, changes do occur in all gardens. There are many causes; some can be controlled, others cannot. Each gardener handles the changes in different ways. Some do not notice the problem until it has destroyed plants. When plants die some gardeners just leave the vacant spots and try to ignore them. Others give up gardening altogether. Still others accept what they cannot change and change what they can in order to continue having their garden to flourish. How like the gardener we are in life!

As parents of children notice their children grow up and leave home, they are like gardeners. They see major changes occur. They notice vacant spots. They realize some of this could have been prevented or controlled, but others could not. Their reactions are similar to the flower or vegetable gardeners. Some try to ignore it by filling their lives with things that don't matter, becoming selfish and self-centered. Still others withdraw from life and give up. Still others change what can be changed and accept what cannot. They "bloom where they are planted" and help others to do the same.

If a mother allows selfishness or apathy to control her life, there will be many empty spots in her personal rose garden. Sadly, the two diseases, like blight on plants in our gardens can quickly spread to endanger others.

Selfishness and apathy, as stated before, are painful and deadly. But, how fortunate we are that they are not like two diseases we hear much of these days, cancer and rheumatoid arthritis. Such is not the case with selfishness and apathy. The cause can be discovered and there is a cure. Before we seek to identify "cause and cure," let's look at the Bible for some ways in which some mothers filled the vacant spots.

A Great Example

Actually we need but one example. It is so complete. That is the example of Mary, the mother of our Lord.

It would be helpful to you to review the life of Christ as recorded in Matthew, Mark, Luke and John . . . because it is from these accounts that we learn what we know of Mary.

Let's begin at the beginning: Look at the events surrounding the birth of Jesus. Mary was young. She was betrothed to Joseph. Try to imagine how YOU would feel to discover that you had been chosen to become the mother of a Son who would save the world! His birth exemplified the statement found in Luke 1:37: "For with God nothing shall be impossible." She didn't argue, worry, fret — she put her trust in God.

Then think of the events surrounding the birth — the journey from Nazareth to Bethlehem; no room in the inn; giving birth in a stable; the threat of Herod; the visit of the wise men; all the other events that surrounded the birth. Try to imagine how you would have reacted. All indications are that Mary sought only to do what God told her to do — she trusted Him completely.

We note further, (Luke 2:52) "And Jesus increased in wisdom and stature, and in favour with God and man." To me this reflects the fact that Mary was a good mother who helped her child to grow in the ways that God intended him to grow. Mothers of today have the same challenge. To meet such a challenge means that a mother must be very close to that child. There is a strong bond between them.

But let's look further at Mary. In Luke 2 when Mary and Joseph went to Jerusalem "after the custom of the feast" they took Jesus with them. He was then twelve.

This was the beginning of the "empty nest" in Mary's life. Read Luke 2:42-52. Jesus was lost from Mary and Joseph for three days in a strange city. No, they were lost from Him. What a lesson for us here! We must not become lost from our children, whatever their age. How sad it is to see modern-day mothers (by their example) failing to help their children "be about their Father's business." When Joseph and Mary rebuked Jesus for not being with them, he said (verse 49): "And He said unto them, 'How is it that ye sought me? Wist ye not that I must be about my Father's business?' " Even at this early age, Jesus was showing his earthly parents that God was first in his life. What if Mary had "fallen apart" from the empty nest syndrome? Read verses 50 and 51. Note a number of things:

(1)   Jesus continued to be obedient to his earthly parents;

(2)   Mary and Joseph didn't understand what it was all about; but

(3)   "His mother kept all these sayings in her heart."

Try to imagine how you, as a mother, would have felt if your son had lived the life that Jesus lived on this earth. How would you have handled it? Would you have been angry and become selfish or apathetic?

What about Mary? She was human as you and I are, so we know that she felt sorrow and heartache, and she must have felt pride in Jesus, yet she untied the apron strings. What did she do?

I believe the most outstanding example of how she handled the "empty nest syndrome" is found in the book of John. Read the first five verses of Chapter 2. Here at the marriage in Cana, Jesus performs the first miracle. His mother is there. Can't you relate to her wishing to be helpful so that everything would go well? She said to Jesus "they have no wine." Now, honestly, how would you have reacted to the reply which Jesus made, if YOUR son had said to you as you tried to be helpful: "Jesus saith unto her, Woman, what have I to do with thee? Mine hour is not yet come."

What beautiful words Mary uttered: "Whatsoever he saith unto you, do it." Mary knew that her son was to be the Saviour of the world — God had told her. But do you think that kept her from the normal feelings a mother has toward a child? I think not. It was just that she knew how to handle a matter even as great as this.

As we read of different times when she was in the crowd near Jesus, can't you imagine her heartache when Jesus was doubted, even by his own brothers?

Christ shows each of us a much-needed lesson: God and our spiritual family have a priority rating in our lives and sometimes this makes it necessary to place less importance on the family relationship of our earthly family.

Read this account from Matthew 12:46-50. "While he yet talked to the people, behold, his mother and his brethren stood without, desiring to speak with him. Then one said unto him, Behold, thy mother and thy brethren stand without, desiring to speak with thee. But he answered and said unto him, "Who is my mother, and who are my brethren?" And he stretched forth his hand toward his disciples and said, "Behold my mother and my brethren! For whosoever shall do the will of my Father which is in heaven, the same is my brother and sister and mother."

If there is doubt that Jesus felt any love for Mary, as his mother, that can be dispelled by reading John 19:26-27.

What's A Mother to Do?

Mothers can learn some great lessons from a study of the little that is said of Mary in the Bible.

1. Teach your children well what God wants them to do.

2. Put your trust in God.

3. Accept the things that cannot be changed.

4. When your child leaves home, ask yourself if this is a part of God's plan for the family or something you should have tried to prevent.

But as modern-day mothers we need to do more than just look at Mary's life; we need to make the words of Mary a motto for rearing our children: "Whatsoever he saith unto you, do it." God's Word gives us guidance and direction. It will enable us to know God's will for our lives and our children's lives. It will enable us to identify the cause of the sins of selfishness and apathy and prescribe the infallible cures for both. It will also enable us to know what we can change and what we can't — what we would try to change and what we shouldn't. So the place to begin, if we are to bloom where we are planted in spaces left empty, is with a study of, belief in, and obedience to God's Word.

The second step is to realize the power of prayer. Selfishness keeps us from the place of prayer and so does apathy. Lack of prayer in our lives is, in a sense, pushing God out of our lives, and that leaves a huge vacant spot in our heart's garden.

The third step is to realize that growing toward maturity is God's plan for each of us, both children and parents. When a child leaves home (for college, career, marriage) if parents have done their homework well they need not feel an emptiness. They have taught their children and helped them to mature as Jesus did — mentally, physically, spiritually, and socially. They are ready to fill the roles God has planned for them. The changing roles of children and parents need not mean a separation that isolates one from the other. We can always keep the ties that bind a family together intact, even though they may stretch in different directions.

After I married and left home, I appreciated my mother's response to my leaving. Her continued contact by her letters and phone calls and her encouragement and shared wisdom, when I asked for them, were important to me. She faced the death of a husband, a son's leaving for college, and the marriage of a daughter who moved away, in a short span of time, but she filled the empty spaces we left. She did this by forgetting self in the interest of others and by being involved and not withdrawing.

The fourth step is to count blessings. What if that child who married and left an empty space had been so physically and/or mentally handicapped that it would be impossible for it to ever leave home except to go into an institution. How blessed you are!

The fifth step is to look around for ways to fill the empty spot in your garden.

The sixth step is to look forward. Think about the time when your child will finish college, when you will have grandchildren, when they will return for a visit. Mix these forward looks with a blend of memories of the days gone by. Use that as a spray for the diseases of selfishness and apathy and then live for today, with your eye on the goal of heaven.

Seventh, never miss an opportunity to share a bouquet from your heart's garden with your child and his or her spouse.

FOR THOUGHT AND DISCUSSION

Discuss how selfishness and apathy can be painful and deadly.

Discuss how many others we may affect adversely if we are selfish or apathetic.

Think of someone you know who has handled the "empty nest" well and note some of the things she has done to cope with the situation and bloom where she is planted, filling these empty spaces.

Name some things one might do to fill the vacant spots left when the nest becomes empty.

FOR YOUR PERSONAL USE

Spend some EXTRA time reading your Bible. Share with someone else something you learn or something that helps you to mature with someone else.

Pray.

Go visit someone. Spend some time during the visit talking about the Bible and the ability of the scriptures to encourage, comfort and strengthen us. Pray with that person.

If you know people who are, for the first time, facing the empty nest, go visit them, invite them into your home. Help them to see that as their children leave home, if they have done a good job in "bringing them up in the nurture and admonition of the Lord," that the influence of the parents does not remain within four walls. It reaches into many areas.

When you are feeling "empty" in that empty nest or cheated and you feel like giving in to selfishness or apathy, read John 3:16. Think about Mary. Then ask yourself, "Do I really have a problem, or have I just been looking for an excuse to turn my back on God?"

MY PRAYER FOR YOU

Dear loving, Heavenly Father: Teach us to love as you have loved us.

When we turn our backs on you, please turn us around that we may move in the right direction — TOWARD Thee and not AWAY from Thee.

Help us to realize that as our children mature according to Your plan, so must we continue to mature as Your children.

Keep us, Father, from the pain and destruction that our selfishness and apathy could cause us and others.

Help us to realize that with You as our Father and Christ as our Saviour, the gardens of our hearts can always bloom abundantly - even in empty spaces. But help us to realize, also, that this growth is only possible when we are willing to nurture our gardens by YOUR plan.

May we bask in Your love and grace and so bloom where we are planted. In Jesus' Name.

Amen

CHAPTER 12

BLOOM WHERE YOU ARE PLANTED IN YOUR GOLDEN YEARS

Introduction:

Since I am on the shady side of seventy, I feel qualified to write on this subject, although I must confess I do not feel like a "golden ager."

From my personal observances, it appears there is a fairly wide spread tendency to group those 65 and over into a conglomerate group and call them " the elderly," "senior citizens," or "those in their golden years." The names do not bother me. The groupings do. Just because a person is a certain age does not mean that person is like every other person of the same age. This is true within every age group.

If I were to generalize, I would say that those past 65 are different from one another in these ways:

(1) Health or physical condition

(2) Mental capacity or alertness

(3) Spiritual growth

(4) Attitudes

(5) Zest for life, both here and hereafter.

So we need to see ourselves and others as "individuals" and not as "groups."

The purpose of this chapter is for us to look at the scriptures and also the practical side of life to determine (from a close look at the five items mentioned above) how we can bloom where we are planted, even in our golden years.

A Rose is a Rose is a Rose

Have you ever noticed how different flowers of the same family can be? One poinsettia may bloom profusely after it is delivered by the florist; another may begin shedding its bright colored petals and leaves immediately.

A rose bud does not remain a rosebud forever. It begins to open up and becomes more fragrant, more open, and at times, more beautiful. It is still a rose. In time, it begins to shed its petals slowly. Finally, when all the petals are gone, we say it has withered and died. But it is still a rose. Are we so different?

I like to think of those in the golden years of life as being roses in full bloom, not as those that have withered and died. We still have a spiritual fragrance, and we still have something to contribute to the world around us — a beauty all our own. As Christian women, inner beauty becomes more radiant with each passing year; it does not fade — it glows.

Even after a rose has shed its petals, its memory remains. How many women have a pressed rose from a first date or their wedding bouquet. So it is as we grow older. If our life has been a radiant Christian life, it will leave memories, influences, and fragrances that will bring joy and happiness to others long after we are gone.

But a rose, whether it is a bud or a full bloom, is still a rose. So it is with a person; a person is a person is a person and deserves to be treated as such as long as he or she lives.

Yet society (and we, ourselves) often tend to put those who have reached the golden years on a shelf and commit them to a life of feeling useless and unneeded. It is true that I cannot do what I did when I was 20. It is equally true that there are some things I can do now that I never could have done when I was 20.

There is a need for looking closely at what those in their golden years can add to the world around them and then providing the opportunities, and encouraging the golden agers to grasp the opportunities, that they may continue to grow.

I Read It In My Bible

One has but to look at the scriptures to discover that aging is a part of God's plan for our lives. In Ecclesiastes, the third chapter, we find the words, "To everything there is a season and a time to every purpose under the heaven." Our lives are so like the seasons — Spring, Summer, Autumn and Winter — they each serve a purpose, so we should not rebel against them.

Each person knows that as the years pass there are visible changes in our physical being. Sometimes these are very difficult to handle. Sometimes they may leave us incapable of handling our own needs. As the theme runs throughout the Bible, God's world and God's plan for our lives is one of "balance." So as we enter the golden age period of life, we need to recognize what we can do and what we can't. We do not need to try to be a rosebud when time calls for us to be full bloom. Nor do we need to wither and die just because we have become a full-blown rose. Ecclesiastes 12 gives some advice to the young in the first verse and then follows with a vivid description of the changes that take place in our lives as we age. Note the last two verses which provide a key to balancing our lives (young or old): "Let us hear the conclusion of the whole matter; Fear God, and keep his commandments: for this is the whole duty of man. For God shall bring every work into judgment, with every secret thing, whether it is good, or whether it be evil." Whatever our age, it is good to serve the Lord in the ways in which we can; it is evil to seek to avoid that which we can do to serve. If our lives are to be "balanced," they must include some service to God and fellowman. May each of us learn to say sincerely, as did the Apostle Paul, "I have learned in whatsoever state I am, therewith to be content."

Search the scriptures and find three examples (men or women) who found ways to serve the Lord even in their old age. Then discuss the ways in which they served. Were they all the same? Was each different from the other? How? Is there any record of what they did in their youth and what they did in their later years? What were the differences in their opportunities.

Read Titus 2 and think about how it applies to those in their golden years. Does God put them on a shelf and expect them to be and to feel useless and unneeded? Instead, I read these words as a strong challenge.

Psalm 90:9 reads, in part, ". . . we spend our days as a tale that is told." What should concern us is what kind of tale is our life reflecting. Will it be of value or idle nonsense? Have you ever read a continued story in a magazine and waited breathlessly for the conclusion. When it came, the ending of the story was so weak that you felt, not only disappointed, but also cheated? We write our life's story each day we live, and, unless we are writing it by God's plan the end of our lives will be weak and without hope. We need to say with the Psalmist, "So teach us to number our days that we may apply our hearts unto wisdom." (Psalm 90:12).

The golden years are a part of God's plan for our lives. He intends for us to bloom where we are planted, and He is always with us. Psalm 46:1 says, "God is our refuge and strength, a very present help in trouble." So if we are having a problem coping with growing older, we need to lean on and trust in our Lord.

My husband, Charles, and I sometimes present workshops having to do with the value of the elderly to the work of the church. Each workshop looks at the matter from two vantage points: (1) What the church programs can do to involve the elderly and (2) what the elderly have to offer and to gain from remaining active, interested, and useful as they continue their spiritual growth.

We are also doing research for a book we hope to write on the subject. The idea for the book came when we heard a sermon entitled "Slaying Lions in the Midst of Pits in Time of Snow." taken from II Samuel 23:20. Sometimes as we grow older, this may be the way we see our lives — in the midst of pits in time of snow. May God give us the strength, wisdom, courage, and enthusiasm to slay the lions wherever they are found.

One of the lions those in the golden years find they must sometimes slay is the lion of loneliness. My good friend, Dr. Al Price, professor at Freed-Hardeman College, suggests one read II Timothy. 4:9-22 and look closely at what it says about the problem of loneliness with which the Apostle Paul grappled. Then he offers "four ways to take the lone out of loneliness."

1. Invest in time with intimate friends (v. 9,11,21).
2. Take care of yourself (v. 13).
3. Spend some time with the scriptures (v. 13).
4. Focus on our future with God (v. 6-8, 18)

I would add one more — find some kind of service (no matter how small) that you can render and do it, giving God the glory.

One might take the words GOLDEN YEARS and look at some wonderful tools for use in slaying lions in the midst of pits in time of snow:

G   Growing spiritually as long as we live.
O   Optimism that enables us to see through the troubles to the silver linings.
L   Love for God and fellowman that outweighs love of self.
D   Dedication to and dependence on God.
E   Enthusiasm for the Christian life.
N   Never giving up.

Y   Yearning for heaven.
E   Edifying others in both words and deed.
A   Always taking time to count one's blessings.
R   Reaching out to others in love.
S   Staying in touch with God through study and prayer.

You Can Do It!

Look around you at the older women you know. What are they doing? Ask yourself from what your greatest hindrance to serving and being involved stems. Is it lack of self-confidence, fear of failure, being unwilling to do what you can instead of what you USED to do, being unable to find an outlet for your talents, not feeling physically capable of doing anything, looking at the many you know who are not involved in serving the Lord and their fellowman and saying, "If they don't, why should I?"

For this portion of this chapter, I shall merely list some things women from 65 through their late 90's are doing to serve the Lord. Notice the difference in what they are doing; yet if their attitude is right, they are doing it to glorify God and not for self-glory. They can be assured it is pleasing to God. The fringe benefit is that their older years are truly golden.

They Bloom Where They Are Planted

1. She has cancer and has to remain in bed most of the time and is often in severe pain. She is an avid reader and clips items she thinks her minister or Bible teachers could use and mails them.

2. She is in her nineties and shut-in. The leaders asked her to write notes to all visitors to the church. Someone brings them by on Monday and she works all week on them.

3. She has taught and written material for small children for years. Now she is preparing material and hopes to be helping younger women learn how to teach children's Bible classes. In recent years she went to Brazil to teach in a Vacation Bible School.

4. She is an outstanding Bible scholar who possesses an unbelievable humility. Her example has touched more lives than can be counted.

5. She is a shut-in, but she telephones absentees.

6. She is retired, but she provides transportation for others, prepares meals for the sick, and serves in whatever capacity she is able.

7. She has artistic abilities, so she prepares visual aids for Bible teachers.

8. She reads for the blind.

9. She has learned the sign language and interprets for the deaf.

10. She invites one or two young people into her home for cookies and milk and they love it.

11. She maintains an active prayer list and prays regularly for those on the list.

12. With the help of a young mother, who is her neighbor, she conducts a neighborhood Bible story hour for neighborhood youngsters once a week.

The list is endless, but these may stimulate our thinking so that we may find more ways in which to serve.

One thing that will help each of us to bloom where we are planted in our golden years is to realize that God does not measure our service against that of others, as we are often prone to do. God does not expect of us the impossible. Yet how often the things that seem impossible to us at the moment, with God's help become not only possibilities, but also realities.

Romans 12:1 says, "I beseech you therefore, brethren, by the mercies of God, that ye present your bodies a living sacrifice, holy, acceptable unto God, which is your reasonable service."

Read Romans 12 and 13 and find verses that could help each of us to bloom where we are planted in our golden years.

The more I read and study and observe the area of "service," the more I realize our need to view it in its true sense. We know that we cannot work our way to heaven, so it should not be viewed as a checklist for which we gain brownie points. We know that 'service' is not limited to planned church programs, so we need to be on the alert for opportunities to serve. We know from the scriptures, such as Romans 12 and the parable of the talents, that we do not all have the same talents, so it is important that we learn how to use those that we possess personally. It is important to learn to develop new talents. But we know God is displeased when we hide or bury our talents. We need to see serving as a privilege granted us to become the hands, feet, ears, eyes and voices of Jesus in the work he began here on earth, while he is in Heaven preparing our mansions, and that is not a burden or a duty, but a special privilege afforded us as Christians. We also need to see serving as a way in which we can follow our Master's example of "ministering to others."

When service becomes something we do from hearts of love and something in which we find a deep and abiding joy, then we can bloom where we are planted, whatever our age.

My own life has been enriched by three women who, in their golden years, shared with me their wisdom and their example - my own mother, the late Vida Pittman Barnett; Manilla Sparks of Gadsden, Alabama; and Louise Dixon of Henderson, Tennessee. They always had time for me, and to discuss the Bible with them was and remains one of the greatest growth experiences of my life. My prayer is that my area of service will follow the same paths.

FOR THOUGHT AND DISCUSSION

1. In your own area what are some means that are available and possible for those in their golden years for service in the church in the community, or in other ways?

2. List some hindrances to women's being involved in service when they reach the golden years?

3. What are some ways in which those hindrances or obstacles could be overcome?

4. In the congregation where you worship, what could be done to encourage and make it possible for the "golden agers" to bloom where they are planted in the field of service.

FOR YOUR PERSONAL USE

1. List three talents you possess (anything from baking a good apple pie to teaching a Bible class or hosting a home Bible study). Whatever YOUR talent is, list it.

   1. _____

   2. _____

   3. _____

2. Now pray to God that you may find ways to use that talent to glorify Him.

3. Now during this week find some way to use each of the talents you listed. Do that each week for a month and you will find it has become easier and easier to do.

4. Find a picture of a beautiful rose and paste it at the top of a sheet of plain paper. Each time you have "bloomed where you are planted," write on this paper. Then take time to thank God for the opportunity you have had.

MY PRAYER FOR YOU

Our loving Heavenly Father, we need Thee every hour, especially in our golden years. Please be with us.

May it be, Father, that we may still see and hear opportunities to serve although our sight and hearing may not be as strong as in our youth.

Give us strength, wisdom and courage to serve in simple ways as our bodies become more frail.

And, dear Father, help us not to "keep score" as we are so often prone to do: "I did this for her and she's never done for me." Instead, let us realize that no matter how great our service, it can never be even a small measure of the love you have shown for us.

May we realize, Father, that each time we bloom where we are planted, we may be encouraging a younger woman to bloom where SHE is planted.

We love you, God; help us to show that love in expressions of love to others. In Jesus' name.

Amen

PART III
HOW DOES YOUR GARDEN GROW?

LIFE'S GOALS
by Louise Barnett Cox

What is the goal in life I seek?
    Whatever do I call my aim?
Could it be wealth? or maybe pow'r
    or is it earthly fame?

May these my goals forever be. . . .
    to LIVE, to LOVE, to LEAVE. . . .
(And ne'er by tho't or word or deed
    Give to others cause to grieve).

For one to LIVE for Christ
    Is to claim a wealth untold
That can ne'er be measured by
    One's silver or one's gold.

If I can truly LOVE mankind
    'Twill lie within my pow'r
To share with all mankind
    Its finest or its darkest hour.

And if I LEAVE the world some better
    Because I walked this way,
"Twas good that she has been here"
    is all that folks need say.

For if I seek these special goals
    LIVE, LOVE and LEAVE - these three
Then I shall surely claim Christ's promise
    That I should live abundantly.

CHAPTER 13

WHAT LACK I YET?

Introduction:

The purpose of this chapter is to serve as a review of HEART'S BOUQUET and also as a self-examination of our own heart's garden.

If this is used as a classroom study, have different women lead a discussion on each of the first six chapters. If possible choose someone in each of the categories discussed in chapters 7 through 12. The discussion should be an open one with a careful look at what we need to do to bloom where we are planted and at how to plan, prepare, plant, weed, and water our own personal gardens. Each woman in the class should have something special to share.

If this is to be used as a private study, then look back over the book and note the chapters that discuss a special need that you have. Study them, Bible in hand, and pray that God will give you both a submissive heart and a servant's heart. Without an attitude of both submission and service we can have no flowers to share from our Heart's Bouquet. And how the world needs all the Heart's Bouquets it can get!

Am I Growing!

A rose bush that is not growing will never have blossoms to share. A Christian woman who feels there is no need for continuing spiritual growth will never be able to bloom where she is planted. So we need to ask ourselves (and answer sincerely), "Do I lack spiritual growth?"

Fleshly Versus Spiritual

If most women who read this book were asked to check this list found in Galatians 5:19-21 and Revelation 21:8, they would say that these were not problems for them. Look at the list:

FROM GALATIANS 5:19-22

Adultery	Wrath
Fornication	Strife
Uncleanness	Seditions
Lasciviousness	Heresies
Idolatry	Envyings
Witchcraft	Murders
Hatred	Drunkenness
Variance	Revellings
Emulations	

FROM REVELATION 21:8

Fearful	Sorcerers
Unbelieving	Idolaters
Abominable	All liars
Murderers	

Read these scriptures and see what is the fate of those who do such things.

As we look at these lists, it is often easy to feel very comfortable. We may even feel good about ourselves as compared to others. This is a soil in which self-righteousness is easily grown. Perhaps there is no disease more threatening to our heart's garden than self-righteousness.

Look at how much such an idea is opposed to the scriptures: Galatians 6:1: "Brethren, if a man be overtaken in a fault, ye which are spiritual, restore such an one in the spirit of meekness; considering thyself, lest thou also be tempted."

Romans 12:3: "For I say, through the grace giveth unto me, to every man that is among you, not to think of himself more highly than he ought to think; but to think soberly, according as God hath dealt to every man the measure of faith."

How much (and this cannot be stressed too often) we need the attitude of the Apostle Paul who said in Philippians 3:13-14; "Brethren, I count not myself to have apprehended: but this one thing I do, forgetting those things which are behind and reaching forth unto those things which are before, I press toward the mark for the prize of the high calling of God in Christ Jesus."

The mathematics of Christian living is both subtraction and addition. Certainly we must subtract those things that separate us from God. But we cannot stop there. We must add other things to our lives. It is often with the addition that we, as Christians, have the greatest problems. Let's go back to two scriptures we've just read;

Galatians 5:22-23: "But the fruit of the Spirit is love, joy, peace, long-suffering, gentleness, goodness, faith, meekness, temperance; against such there is no law."

How can we think more highly of ourselves than we should if any of these qualities are present in our lives. It is not enough to be against evil, we must also reflect good.

II Peter 1:5-7 points out the growth needed to keep the gardens of our heart blooming abundantly: "And beside this, giving all diligence, add to your faith virtue; and to virtue knowledge; and to knowledge temperance; and to temperance patience; and to patience godliness; and to godliness brotherly kindness; and to brotherly kindness charity (or love)."

Compare verses 8 and 9 and see what the end results of growing and not growing are. If our heart's gardens are dead or filled with diseased plants we have no bouquet to share.

Read the all-familiar 13th Chapter of I Corinthians. Does this help us to realize that what we do or refrain from doing must be more than a sort of computerized programming? Our actions must stem from a heart of love. Many people can "put up a good front," and pretend to be all that God intends them to be, but still be deceitful. But God knows the condition of the soil in our heart's gardens and God knows what kind of flowers bloom there. God also knows when we share a bouquet whether it is shared with the right attitude or with strings attached.

Looking at this chapter further, let's check some ways in which we may determine that we are serving and sharing from a love of God and mankind, or whether it is for self-glory. Paul in this chapter says of love:

It suffers long (is patient),
Is kind,
Does not envy,
Does not vaunt itself (has humility),
Is not puffed up (not self-righteous among other things),
Doesn't behave itself unseemly,
Doesn't seek its own,
Is not easily provoked,
Thinketh no evil,
Rejoiceth not in iniquity,
Rejoiceth in truth,
Beareth all things,
Believeth all things,
Hopes and endures all things.

Think how much better the world would be and how beautiful the bouquets from our heart's gardens would become if only you and I practiced these qualities in all our dealings.

It is said that communication is the world's biggest problem. Discuss how having these qualities would make communication less difficult.

It is also said that "If our relationship with God is right, there is no way it can be wrong with our fellowman." Then discuss this. If our relationship with our fellowman is wrong in any way, is there any way it can be right with God?

Searching Deeper

As we have looked at the addition and the subtraction needed in Christian living, I hope we have also discovered that when we share our joys and our hope, we multiply them. When we divide the burdens of others among ourselves, we reduce them. God never asks of us anything that is not for OUR good.

Christ was perfect. He is our example. But in our enthusiasm to be like Jesus Christ, we must realize that perfection will not be found on earth. It is something we must continue to strive for as long as we live.

Yet how often we demand perfection of ourselves and others. If God had expected perfection, He would not have provided an avenue of forgiveness for either the alien sinner nor the erring Christian. How can we put ourselves above God in demanding perfection of anyone and refusing to forgive?

The Wisdom of the Young

When I discussed this chapter with a group of young women, one of them had this to say:

"I know what I lack. I believe it is a lack that many people have. Even when we are doing what God wants us to do, we are often seeking the praise of men, rather than striving to please God. We may be trying to win the approval of our parents, a dedicated Christian friend, the preacher, the elders, our Bible teacher. We are doing what God says to do, in part, but we have lost sight of our need to please God with our very lives."

FOR THOUGHT AND DISCUSSION

1. Is it easy or difficult to face up to the question "What Lack I Yet?" Why?

2. Make a list of things of which God does not approve, look at them carefully and discuss which is the most prevalent in the world today. In the church. What outside influences have a direct effect on these qualities in our lives?

3. Which of the qualities we SHOULD have in our lives is the most difficult to come by. Why?

4. In which area of our lives (home, work, community, church) are the good qualities most difficult to achieve? Why?

5. Which of the list is the easiest for you to practice regularly? Why?

6. Why does the quality of LOVE make our service and our sharing of our Heart's Bouquets more beautiful?

FOR YOUR PERSONAL USE

Decide what it is you lack and then work on the problem. Look at all the difficulties your lack of that quality has caused you. Look at why your life and those around you would be better if you acquired that trait.

My greatest lack is PATIENCE, both with myself and with others. I pray to God for help in overcoming this lack. In His wisdom, God gives me many situations that truly try my patience, and I can see that I am (slowly) gaining more patience.

Perhaps you know someone who has the quality you lack. Get to know that person and ask how they have achieved that special quality in their lives.

The most important move any of us can make to insure abundant blossoms in our heart's garden is to put our total trust in God and God's Word in every situation. When we come to realize fully that God's way is always best, even though we may not be able to see it at that moment, we can trust him. When we accept the fact that His grace is sufficient for us, then we can be at peace, but we will always want to keep growing spiritually.

I wish each of us could learn to talk about Jesus as easily as we talk about recipes. fashion, TV. shows, etc. Nothing is more comforting, joyful and beautiful than just talking simply about what Jesus means in our lives. Yet we do it so seldom.

A FINAL THOUGHT

My prayer is that this book will help each person who reads it to grow closer to God and to share the beauty of Jesus' love with others. It has helped me. May it help you also. For as we grow spiritually, others benefit from our growth as do we.

The following poem was given me by my friend, Rosemary McKnight. It reflects so beautifully the acceptance of God's plan for our lives so that we may share our Heart's Bouquets as long as we live and after we are gone.

The poem was written by Kayla Ann Jestice, a Christian young woman, graduate of Oklahoma Christian College, who died at age 30. The poem was found in her personal possessions. Her parents, Lee and Shirley Jestice, Miami, OK, have given me permission to use the poem, for which I am grateful.

GOD'S GARDEN

God works in His garden
I'm told every day:
With the roses He needs,
For His heavenly bouquet.

There are times when he picks
All the withered, the old,
And gathers them lovingly
Into his fold.

There are times when He prunes
Where some others must grow,
That He on the weak ones
More strength may bestow.

But some days he chooses
The fairest in sight;
He needs certain buds
To make heaven look right.

How sweet, oh, how beautiful
Is His bouquet.
God works in His garden
And best is His way.

Kayla Ann Jestice

As I talked with Kayla's mother, I found that she was a young woman who did not let difficult circumstances prevent her from "blooming where she was planted." The fragrance of the blossoms from her Heart's Bouquet continue to enrich the lives of people who knew her and also those who never met her.

If Kayla could do it, so can we. Let's bloom where we are planted and share as many of our heart's bouquets as we can during our life on this earth. All it takes is a deep faith in God and a loving relationship with Jesus and a sincere concern for the welfare (both physical and spiritual) of those around us.

CONCLUSION

As you finish this book and think seriously about your Heart's Bouquet, I would like to share with you a true story of some lessons I learned from a crocus.

The crocus is my favorite flower. When we lived in Cartersville, Georgia, we always planted them near our back door and down the edge of our drive which sloped into the street. I watched for them eagerly each year.

At the end of the drive that led into the street was a clump of the most stubborn weeds I have ever seen. Nothing we did would get rid of them. I disliked them as much as I liked the crocus.

It was a late spring and the crocus had not bloomed. I was impatient. As we drove out of the drive one morning, Charles called my attention to the clump of weeds. There in those weeds bloomed the first crocus of the season. . . how beautiful it was.

What lessons? That little crocus didn't care if the weeds were stubborn. It bloomed anyway. It didn't care if it was the only crocus blooming. It bloomed anyway. It didn't wait for ideal circumstances. It bloomed anyway. It didn't fear the chill that was in the air. It just lifted its face to the sun and bloomed away. So can you and I lift our faces to the SON and bloom anyway, despite stubborn influences of the world and less than ideal circumstances. If we are the only ones willing to bloom, and even if we get a cold shoulder from those around us, if we lift our faces to the Son we can bloom anyway. And what lovely blooms we'll share from our heart's gardens!

CPSIA information can be obtained at www.ICGtesting.com
Printed in the USA
LVOW060459040613

336840LV00001B/1/P